ALSO BY HANNAH PITTARD

Visible Empire

Listen to Me

Reunion

The Fates Will Find Their Way

WE
ARE
TOO
MANY

WE ARE TOO MANY

A Memoir
[Kind of]

Hannah Pittard

Henry Holt and Company
New York

Henry Holt and Company
Publishers since 1866
120 Broadway
New York, New York 10271
www.henryholt.com

Henry Holt® and ⓗ are registered trademarks of Macmillan Publishing
Group, LLC.

Library of Congress Cataloging-in-Publication Data is available.

ISBN: 9781250869043

Our books may be purchased in bulk for promotional, educational,
or business use. Please contact your local bookseller or the Macmillan
Corporate and Premium Sales Department at (800) 221-7945, extension
5442, or by e-mail at MacmillanSpecialMarkets@macmillan.com.

First Edition 2023

Designed by Meryl Sussman Levavi

Printed in the United States of America

10 9 8 7 6 5 4 3 2 1

For Elmer, who was a very good dog

And for Jeff, who lets me keep it weird

Now women find that they need more than one man in a lifetime. We're each too many people for one mate to satisfy. Look at the symbols of man and woman—the man's arrow points up because he isn't monogamous, he wants to screw and move on. But I'm not sure women don't want exactly the same thing. If they do bend aside and choose one man, in order to make it work over a long period of time, they've got to be very very independent and have, not affairs necessarily, but . . .

—from *Talk*, Linda Rosenkrantz

If you don't change with the times, . . . the times are going to change you.

—Marv Levy, former head coach of the Buffalo Bills

WE
ARE
TOO
MANY

INTRODUCTION

This book began as a response to a question frequently posed to me by readers of an essay that I wrote for Adam Ross and the *Sewanee Review* in 2017. In the essay, I discussed my husband's affair with my best friend, and I confessed to having previously mined my own failing marriage for material for my third novel, which tells the story of a couple in crisis.

The confession came naturally, in part, because it wasn't the first time I'd cannibalized my life for material. In grad school, my peers constantly accused me of writing personal essays disguised as fiction by way of the third-person pronoun. "This is you," they'd say. "This is you. This is you. This is you." Except on one occasion, when I wrote about an intimate revelation regarding a classmate's husband, one she'd made a few weeks earlier, over drinks, and to several members of the workshop. "This is me," the classmate said bluntly, and everyone in the room, most especially me, marveled with disappointment at my overstep.

Later, thinking I'd learned my lesson and while writing my first novel, I stole heavily from my childhood—but from *my* memories of my childhood: of basement antics and pool party pranks and locker room gossip. I stole from remembered conversations—sometimes overheard and often misperceived—as well as from the shameless rumors we children told and retold about ourselves and each other, each recitation enjoying a new embellishment courtesy of our youthful imaginations—imaginations that had no anchor in honesty or ownership.

This sort of cannibalistic approach to fiction comes with its fair share of interpersonal risk. In 2011, my grandfather killed himself on a back porch in Atlanta, and that suicide became the inciting incident for my second novel. There are people who have never forgiven me for the trespass. Nor am I alone in my intrusions into the lives of those close to me: Joseph Heller famously alienated his children, who accused him of lifting their conversations with him verbatim. ("What makes you think you're interesting enough to write about?" was his response.) James Salter based the central characters of his masterpiece *Light Years* on a pair of dear friends, shocking them upon the book's publication. There is always the danger, of course, that writers will become ensnared by the autobiographical details they are trying to use and misperceive the truth.

This may or may not have been the case with my third novel, which was published the same week I discovered my husband's affair with my best friend. In many ways, I felt the ultimate failure was mine: over the course of several years, I chose to focus on my art instead of on my marriage. Though my husband was the one to cheat, I was not entirely blameless. My disloyalty to our union—privileging our conversations as fodder for material, for instance, rather than investing in them as a means to repair—preceded his own.

For nearly a year after my divorce, I worked on the *Sewanee* essay with Adam, and the process was an undeniably therapeutic one. By the time it was published, I felt I'd turned a corner: I didn't cry when my ex-husband called me; I didn't cry when I cooked dinner alone; I didn't cry when my mother asked if I was eating enough or working out too much or if I'd started vomiting again. I didn't even cry on the one occasion I agreed to have drinks with my ex-husband and my former best friend.

By then, I only ever felt a jab of pain when people would ask, having read my essay, "But what's the real story? What really went on between the three of you?" What they wanted to know, as one especially candid reader put it, were "the nasty bits." In other words, they wanted to know the details. But also, I think they wanted to know how those details could be shuffled and reshuffled into the characters' different perceptions of reality. To be honest, so did I.

A healthy habit or not, it's in my nature to play conversations over and over in my head. In the pages that follow are the conversations I remember most vividly from the ten years I spent with my husband. Taking great liberties and very likely getting much of it wrong, these imperfectly recollected exchanges (in person, by phone, and by text) are between my husband, my best friend, my sister, other friends, parents, counselors, and me. Sometimes they are imagined from whole cloth (as when I attempt to reconstruct the discussion between my husband and best friend that might have led to their initial infidelity), and sometimes they are recalled as clearly and honestly as if they'd taken place just last night (as when my husband suggested we have a baby in order to curb our excessive drinking habits). Collectively, these conversations are meant to provide the substance and context of a marriage that was destined to fail from the beginning and a friendship that was doomed to end in betrayal.

What began as a response to curious readers has since morphed into an investigation into the intersection of memory, self, honesty, and personal accounting—an investigation that sharply questions the legitimacy, ownership, and accuracy of personal and shared memories. During our divorce and as we went about the arduous task of uncoupling our lives, my husband and I had plenty of opportunities to argue. We had plenty of opportunities to rehash how and why we'd gotten where we were. Most maddening to me during these arguments—more even than his infidelity—was his insistence on a version of our marriage that completely clashed with mine. Most maddening to him, he told me later, was my unwillingness even to entertain his point of view.

After our divorce, I didn't immediately stop hearing my husband's voice in my head or stop guessing how he might respond to something I'd read or heard or said if he'd still been in the room to hear me say it. I didn't overnight stop thinking of things that might turn him thoughtful or make him laugh. Especially when I took our dog for walks alone, I thought about him, thought about the conversations we *weren't* having; and I allowed myself to invent both sides—not as two people still together, but as two people who'd spent a decade together and who were now suddenly apart. Maybe this is just an elaborate way of admitting that I missed him and that, in missing him, I did what I do naturally: I wrote him down. Without his permission, I re-created him, trying to conjure up this new version of him with which to have a final exchange.

I'm a firm believer that in the particular, we find the universal. In what follows, I've concentrated on a string of echoing events that happened to a particular person, *this* person. But my hope is that by watching one individual's detailed mental maneuvering, readers might begin to ask themselves more intimate and provocative questions about their own decision-making processes and their own relationship to experience, accuracy, and the intentions of memory: Is there a legitimate way to own a recollection? What is a shared memory? When is the personal *too* personal?

N.B.

With the exception of mine, my sister's, Andy's, and the dog's, all the names have been changed. Dates, details, and places have also been altered in some instances.

PART ONE

REMEMBERED CONVERSATIONS

JULY 2016—
HANNAH DISCOVERS HER HUSBAND IS HAVING
AN AFFAIR

Hannah lands in New York City and takes a cab directly from the airport to a northern Thai restaurant, where she meets Hugh, one of her closest friends. They've finished dinner and are now walking back to his apartment. It's that pink time of night.

HUGH: You should ask me questions.

HANNAH: That's a mysterious thing to say.

HUGH: You should be more suspicious.

HANNAH: In general, I would say that I am not a suspicious person.

HUGH: Although in this instance I'm accusing you of not being suspicious enough, I'd argue that you're either lying, delusional, or you have a pretty rotten understanding of your own nature.

HANNAH: You think I'm suspicious?

HUGH: You're paranoid and prone to jealousy.

HANNAH: I agree with that.

HUGH: Where most people assume incompetence, you often assume nefarious intentions.

HANNAH: I have a very keen sense of the world.

HUGH: Ask me a question.

HANNAH: Is this about Patrick?

HUGH: Yes.

HANNAH: Is this about his visit without me to New York last week?

HUGH: Yes.

HANNAH: Did something happen?

HUGH: Yes.

HANNAH: Something bad?

HUGH: I think it's bad.

HANNAH: Did he have sex with someone?

HUGH: Yes.

HANNAH: Did he have sex with Trish?

HUGH: Yes.

HANNAH: You better not be making this up.

JUNE 2016—
ONE WEEK EARLIER, TRISH CALLS HANNAH

Hannah is walking the dog in Lexington, Kentucky. Trish is at a bar in New York City. Patrick is at a writers' retreat in Upstate New York. Temperatures up and down the East Coast are two degrees below normal.

TRISH: I've met someone.

HANNAH: You're always meeting someone.

TRISH: I mean it. He makes me want babies.

HANNAH: Gross.

TRISH: He makes me want to leave my husband.

HANNAH: You say that several times a year.

TRISH: I want him to put babies on me. I'm serious.

HANNAH: Now you sound like your husband. That's something George would say.

TRISH: That's something George *has* said. But this guy makes me *feel* it. I understand what George wants now. But I want it with this other guy instead.

HANNAH: What's his name?

TRISH: He's our age.

HANNAH: Does George know him?

TRISH: George likes him.

HANNAH: Does George know you're having sex? You are having sex with him, aren't you? That's what you mean when you say you've met someone?

TRISH: George knows I'm dating someone.

HANNAH: I don't understand how you can be married and date other people.

TRISH: It's an open marriage.

HANNAH: Since when? You never called it 'open' before. What

about that older man you were seeing? The nightclub owner? What happened to him?

TRISH: This is different. I think I love him.

HANNAH: Huh.

TRISH: Don't be like that.

HANNAH: Like what?

TRISH: Judgmental.

HANNAH: Sorry.

TRISH: Never mind. What about you? How are you? Are you lonely? Do you miss Patrick?

HANNAH: Miss him? He's not dead. He was in France, he was in New York City, and now he's at Yaddo. He'll be back in a month. It feels like the summer is going by too fast. I like being alone.

TRISH: A whole summer apart. I can't imagine.

HANNAH: Says the woman with an ostensibly open marriage.

TRISH: Uh-oh.

HANNAH: What?

TRISH: I smell trouble. What's going on with you two anyway? Are you fighting? Are you unhappy?

HANNAH: We're not anything. We're fine. Did he say something to you when he was in town?

TRISH: We don't talk about things like that.

HANNAH: Huh.

TRISH: You're doing it again.

JULY 2016—
THE MORNING FOLLOWING THE DISCOVERY OF THE AFFAIR, HANNAH CALLS TRISH

Hannah wakes up early and is immediately alert. From the apartment next door, she can hear a man's muffled singing. "Pancho and Lefty"? "Candle in the Wind"? She dials Trish's number.

TRISH: It's early. Are you okay?

HANNAH: It's six a.m. Yeah. It's early. Do you have a minute?

TRISH: You're in the city, right? I'll see you tonight, right?

HANNAH: Can I ask you something?

TRISH: Your book launch party is tonight, isn't it? I have the best outfit.

HANNAH: Quick question.

TRISH: Is everything okay? You sound distracted.

HANNAH: Maybe so. I'm concerned about Patrick.

TRISH: You are?

HANNAH: I am.

TRISH: Why? Has something happened to him?

HANNAH: Do you think something has happened to him?

TRISH: Like what?

HANNAH: I think something really bad has happened to him.

TRISH: Oh my god.

HANNAH: I think he had sex with someone.

TRISH: You do?

HANNAH: Yeah.

TRISH: Why do you think that?

HANNAH: I think he had sex with you.

TRISH: That's crazy.

HANNAH: Did you have sex with him?

TRISH: —

HANNAH: Hello?

TRISH: —

HANNAH: Can you hear me?

TRISH: This is probably a conversation you should be having with your husband.

HANNAH: Please don't use that word with me.

TRISH: What word?

HANNAH: 'Husband.' Are you going to answer my question?

TRISH: You should talk to Patrick.

HANNAH: I'm hanging up.

TRISH: He told me you've always been jealous of me.

HANNAH: It's just like him to get a word wrong. You'll figure that out soon enough. He's smart but not that smart. He's sloppy with language.

TRISH: He says you've always been terrified of this happening.

HANNAH: His memory is even lousier than his vocabulary. I've never *trusted* you. Not trusting a person is different from being jealous.

TRISH: I think he did this on purpose. To drive a wedge between us.

HANNAH: I feel sorry for you.

TRISH: He's a dick.

HANNAH: You're playing this all wrong.

TRISH: I'm not playing.

HANNAH: Thank you for your honesty. I appreciate you telling me the truth.

TRISH: Do you want me to have him call you?

HANNAH: I'm hanging up for real now.

JULY 2016—
SEVERAL HOURS LATER, A PHONE CALL FROM PATRICK

It's early afternoon. Hannah is alone in Hugh's apartment. She feels like a caged animal, pacing and sitting and pacing again, but she knows better than to be caught off guard and in public when Patrick finally calls, which he ultimately does sometime after lunch.

PATRICK: So?

HANNAH: You sound angry.

PATRICK: You talked to Trish?

HANNAH: It's funny that you sound angry. It's also funny that you sound like you just woke up. It's noon. It's past noon.

PATRICK: And?

HANNAH: How hungover are you?

PATRICK: That's your question?

HANNAH: Are you even writing up there? Are you doing anything besides drinking?

PATRICK: Fuck you.

HANNAH: You had sex with Trish?

PATRICK: Yes.

HANNAH: More than once?

PATRICK: Yes.

HANNAH: And you think you're in love?

PATRICK: It's confusing.

HANNAH: Thank you for your honesty. I get the house. I get the car. I get the dog. I'll see a lawyer on Monday.

PATRICK: Did you rehearse that?

HANNAH: I didn't. But it's good, isn't it? I expected to be flustered, but I'm feeling pretty clearheaded at the moment.

PATRICK: We're not going to talk about this?

HANNAH: Did you have sex with Trish?

PATRICK: I told you.

HANNAH: House, car, dog. All mine. Lawyer on Monday.

PATRICK: Fine, then. We can talk about this when I come home.

HANNAH: Home? Home?

PATRICK: My home. Our home.

HANNAH: You don't have a home anymore.

PATRICK: Don't be dramatic. We have a dog!

HANNAH: I have a dog.

PATRICK: You didn't even want to get Elmer!

HANNAH: I can't sleep without him.

PATRICK: Oh, please.

HANNAH: Elmer stays with me.

PATRICK: What about the car?

HANNAH: My car. Dear god, I wish I were recording this. It's going so well.

PATRICK: This is just like you.

HANNAH: What did you expect?

PATRICK: I thought you'd fight. I thought you'd cry.

HANNAH: There are like nine million women you could have had sex with, and we would have worked it out. Cindy in Philosophy. Nancy in Geography. Nine million and twenty-nine women. One billion women. But I've made it incredibly clear from the beginning that there is one woman who is off-limits.

PATRICK: You're so self-righteous. It's disgusting.

HANNAH: I won't have sex with a man who's had sex with Trish. And that doesn't mean I'm jealous of her. It just means I don't trust her.

PATRICK: You're an asshole.

HANNAH: Get a lawyer.

JULY 2016—
PATRICK CALLS TRISH

Trish has taken the day off from work. Patrick is shaken and confused and feels also as though he's isolated from the center of the action, which to his mind is in New York City, which is where his wife and his girlfriend happen to be. He doesn't like their propinquity. He doesn't like how far away he is from either of them.

PATRICK: I'm coming to New York.

TRISH: Good.

PATRICK: I'm leaving this awful place. They're all frauds up here. I need to see you.

TRISH: Yes! I need to see you, too.

PATRICK: I need to figure this out.

TRISH: Yes.

PATRICK: Can I stay with you?

TRISH: Of course.

PATRICK: Did you tell George?

TRISH: I did.

PATRICK: What did he say?

TRISH: He hung up. He didn't believe me at first, and then he hung up. He's probably talking to Hannah now.

PATRICK: Should I call him?

TRISH: Give him time. He'll come around. They both will.

PATRICK: I don't think so. Hannah's mad.

TRISH: She'll get over it.

PATRICK: She says she's seeing a lawyer on Monday. Don't you think that's fast?

TRISH: I think it's good.

PATRICK: Divorce, though? It feels sudden.

TRISH: Do you love me?

PATRICK: I think so.

TRISH: You think so?

PATRICK: I feel muddled.

TRISH: We just blew up our lives. You don't get to feel muddled.

PATRICK: I'm going to the train station now.

TRISH: Good.

PATRICK: I need a drink.

TRISH: Wait until you get here.

PATRICK: I need something to clear my head.

JULY 2016—
HANNAH CALLS HER SISTER

Hannah is alone on the roof of Hugh's apartment building. It's late. She can't sleep. Under the wires and cables and antennae of the city around her, the air is electric.

HANNAH: Guess who's having an affair.

GRETA: Your horrible husband.

HANNAH: Ha! Yes!

GRETA: Wait. For real?

HANNAH: Guess with whom.

GRETA: The loser you insist on referring to as your best friend.

HANNAH: Double ha! Yes, yes!

GRETA: Oh, H . . .

HANNAH: Can you believe it?

GRETA: You sold your MINI for him . . .

HANNAH: The VW is very practical. It has a hatchback.

GRETA: But you loved the MINI. That gorgeous white leather interior . . .

HANNAH: The MINI is long gone.

GRETA: You got him a tenure-track job!

HANNAH: Don't remind me.

GRETA: I've always hated Trish.

HANNAH: Please don't make this about you.

JUNE 2012—
FOUR YEARS EARLIER, PATRICK PROPOSES

Hannah is in the kitchen, one of Patrick's mother's catering aprons tied around her waist. Patrick is at the table, one of Pops's guitars in his hands. Hannah's cooking chili, her only specialty.

PATRICK: Do you want another margarita?

HANNAH: Yes. Here, taste this chili. It's good, right?

PATRICK: Mm.

HANNAH: Less agave next time, though. Also, do you know what I think?

PATRICK: That chili is exceptional, by the way, probably your best yet.

HANNAH: I think you're never going to propose.

PATRICK: I told you: I have a ring.

HANNAH: Sure you do.

PATRICK: It's here. It's in this apartment. It's hidden.

HANNAH: Hidden like the Florentine Diamond.

PATRICK: I don't get the reference.

HANNAH: One hundred and thirty-seven carats.

PATRICK: Do you know what I think? I think you don't actually want to get married.

HANNAH: And I think you only say you want to get married because your dad told you not to fuck things up with me. I think you only want to marry me because you don't want someone else to have me.

PATRICK: You think I'm proposing because of my dad?

HANNAH: I don't think you're proposing.

PATRICK: You know what?

HANNAH: Where are you going?

PATRICK: Just shut up a minute.

HANNAH: Come back in here. Don't shout at me from the bedroom. We don't say 'shut up' in this house.

PATRICK: I wasn't shouting.

HANNAH: We don't say 'shut up.'

PATRICK: I'm sorry. I love you.

HANNAH: I'm sorry I love you, too.

PATRICK: That's funny. Here. Give me your hand.

HANNAH: What is that?

PATRICK: Just take it.

HANNAH: What is this? Christ. What is this?

PATRICK: It's a ring.

HANNAH: Seriously? Right now? You're doing this now? I'm wearing an apron and stirring a pot of chili. You haven't even finished making the margaritas.

PATRICK: Stop stirring the chili and give me an answer.

HANNAH: Did you ask a question?

PATRICK: Will you marry me already?

HANNAH: Duh.

SPRING BREAK 2014—
HANNAH & PATRICK PREPARE TO DRIVE FROM
CHICAGO TO CHARLOTTESVILLE

It's late morning and muggy; cloud ceilings are low all across the country. East of them, a massive storm system is gathering. Neither of them knows it yet, but in approximately twelve hours, they will be spending the night in a hotel without power in the mountains of West Virginia. Hannah is in the kitchen packing a cooler with nuts and fruits and bottles of water. Patrick has just gotten back from walking the dog.

HANNAH: That was fast.

PATRICK: He wouldn't go.

HANNAH: What do you mean, he wouldn't go?

PATRICK: He didn't poop.

HANNAH: If he doesn't poop, then you have to keep walking him. We can't start a twelve-hour drive with a dog who needs to use the bathroom. We'll be stopping in Gary.

PATRICK: What's wrong with stopping in Gary?

HANNAH: Nothing is wrong with stopping in Gary. Except that it'll add another thirty minutes to our drive, and it's almost noon as it is.

PATRICK: It's eleven o'clock.

HANNAH: It's eleven fifteen. I wanted to get in before midnight.

PATRICK: Midnight. The witching hour. When all the bad guys come out to kill you.

HANNAH: I don't see the point of getting started only to have to stop again thirty minutes later and find someplace for him to go.

PATRICK: You think we're going to get carjacked in Gary. Is that it? You think we'll pull off the highway and make a wrong turn and I'll be walking Elmer and some dude will walk up to your window with a gun?

HANNAH: You wouldn't be the one walking him. I'd be the one walking him. When you're tense, he won't go. So I would be the one walking him.

PATRICK: He's a dog.

HANNAH: Dogs have a sense about things. Look at him. He's panting. He's practically drooling.

PATRICK: It's ninety degrees outside.

HANNAH: But it's not ninety degrees in our apartment. He's panting because he's nervous, and he's nervous because you're a dick.

PATRICK: Our dog thinks I'm a dick?

HANNAH: *I* think you're a dick.

PATRICK: So when you're walking Elmer on this alleged side street in Gary, is it me who gets a gun pulled on him or is it you and Elmer?

HANNAH: It's you. You're the one in the car, and you're the one being a dick.

PATRICK: What happens to you?

HANNAH: I get raped.

PATRICK: You have serious issues. You know that, don't you?

HANNAH: Why are you laughing, then?

PATRICK: I'm laughing because I'm married to a lunatic. Tell me what happens to Elmer in this scenario.

HANNAH: Elmer gets stolen. He gets trained up as a fighting dog. He spends the rest of his short life scared and wondering where we are. Wait. What are you doing? Where are you going?

PATRICK: To take him out again.

HANNAH: I'll do it. You don't do it right.

PATRICK: I can't believe I have to be in a car with you for twelve hours.

HANNAH: I can't believe I'm married to you.

PATRICK: Lucky you.

HANNAH: Lucky you.

PATRICK: Lucky me.

HANNAH: Lucky you.

PATRICK: Kiss me.

HANNAH: You're a real dope, you know that?

JULY 2016—
HANNAH CALLS HER SISTER, AGAIN

Hannah is lying on Hugh's air mattress. She's waiting for him to come home so they can go right back out and have a drink before her book launch. She wants to be reckless. She wants to spend money, buy clothes, rack up debt, eat too many slices of pizza, make a scene. Instead, she calls her sister.

HANNAH: They think they're in a Salter novel.

GRETA: I hate her. I've always hated her.

HANNAH: Like, I'm serious. He told me I have no imagination. He compared their love affair to Salter. He used the expression 'love affair.' He said George gets it. He actually told me to be more like George. You know Patrick gave me a copy of a Salter novel before he left for the summer?

GRETA: George is a drunk. Which one?

HANNAH: That's unfortunate but true. You flirted with him once. *Light Years.*

GRETA: I choose to disagree with that statement.

HANNAH: I wish any of this were as interesting as *Light Years.* I wish any of them were as smart as Salter. I wish I were Salter.

GRETA: Salter stole everything from his own life.

HANNAH: He's the one with no imagination.

GRETA: He could write a sentence, though.

HANNAH: I like his use of ellipses.

GRETA: Salter is to ellipsis as Hannah is to em dash.

HANNAH: True.

GRETA: Also *mewl.* Every book of yours, I wait for it, and then there it is. Like Pee-wee Herman's word of the day. I howl whenever I see it.

HANNAH: It's a good word. Say it.

GRETA: Mewl.

HANNAH: Mewl.

GRETA: Mewl.

FALL 2005—
ELEVEN YEARS EARLIER, HANNAH VISITS A GRIEF COUNSELOR

Hannah is sitting on a beige couch, in a beige room, across from a beige lady dressed in beige slacks, and she is counting down the minutes until she can leave. She is wondering if it's rude to leave a counselor's office early. She is wondering if it's rude to say that this whole endeavor was a mistake. She wonders if the counselor takes checks and if there's even enough in her account to cover the cost of this visit. She wonders when, if ever, she will stop writing checks that bounce.

COUNSELOR: I'm thinking Prozac.

HANNAH: Prozac?

COUNSELOR: We'll start you off small.

HANNAH: You think I need Prozac?

COUNSELOR: It's definitely worth a shot.

HANNAH: Because I'm grieving the senseless cruelty of my step-father's diagnosis and his rapid decline?

COUNSELOR: I've had very good luck with Prozac.

FALL 2005—
HANNAH & TRISH DISCUSS LIVE BANDS AND
EATING DISORDERS

They're at a bar. Hannah's just off work. She's dressed all in black, in clothes she bought at Target. She hates the way she smells. Her face is greasy from waiting tables. Trish is in one of her outfits. She is always in an outfit. Her hair is up in an intricate series of braids.

TRISH: You have to come with me to hear this band.

HANNAH: I don't really like live music.

TRISH: That's what you always say. There will be guys there.

HANNAH: My last boyfriend, Stephen Strange, loved music. *Loved* it. For six years, I let him drag me from record shop to record shop. I never told him how much I hated it. One time he defecated in his pants, he was so excited to find some album. Don't laugh. I'm not kidding. We had to leave the store and find a place with a public bathroom where he could take off his boxers and just throw them away. I stayed with him another four years. That's batty, you know. Not because of his accident—I can understand that level of excitement—but because of disliking the things he actively liked. What I mean is, I should probably learn from that experience. Develop a backbone? Not go along with everything just because?

TRISH: When I met you, you were still wearing a jog bra as your daily bra. Also, I love that you never talk about your last boyfriend without saying his full name: Stephen Strange. Where did he finally use the bathroom?

HANNAH: It's a name that begs to be said in full. The only reason you know I wore a jog bra every day is because I told you.

TRISH: Where was the bathroom?

HANNAH: Chipotle. It was my first time in one. I waited in line as though I was going to order something.

TRISH: You didn't have to tell me you only wore jog bras. We could all see. Uniboob.

HANNAH: We?

TRISH: The workshop.

HANNAH: You think anybody in workshop besides you noticed my jog bra?

TRISH: This from the girl who literally thinks everybody is looking at her all the time, when in reality nobody even knows you're in the room.

HANNAH: You've made my point for me. Nobody notices the uniboob of a wallflower.

TRISH: Jesus! I just want you to come hear this band!

HANNAH: Why can't George go?

TRISH: He's bartending. He'll meet us after.

HANNAH: After? I plan to be asleep by ten p.m.

TRISH: How do you expect to get a boyfriend in this town if you insist on going to bed so early?

HANNAH: Who says I want another boyfriend anytime soon?

TRISH: You're such a liar.

HANNAH: I want to *want* to be more independent.

TRISH: The lead singer is dreamy.

HANNAH: 'Dreamy.' Ick.

TRISH: He's fucking sexy.

HANNAH: Why don't you hook up with him, then? Also, isn't he forty years old? Possibly more than forty years old?

TRISH: I have a boyfriend already. I have George. The lead guitarist is cute, too.

HANNAH: 'Cute.' Right up there with 'dreamy.'

TRISH: He plays Scrabble. You'd like him. He's younger. He's our age. I kind of have a crush, actually.

HANNAH: Does George know?

TRISH: You don't even know how sexy you are.

HANNAH: I feel like you're patronizing me. I've gained five pounds since I started grad school.

TRISH: So lose it. You look great. But lose it. I don't disagree that you could and should lose it. But you really are sexy.

HANNAH: Sometimes I wonder why you're so nice to me.

TRISH: Here's something that's not nice: I hate when you're self-deprecating. It's boring.

HANNAH: I don't have anything to wear.

TRISH: Wear what you have on.

HANNAH: These clothes smell.

TRISH: What do they smell like?

HANNAH: Like my job. Like the brunch shift. Like meat loaf.

TRISH: You're going to have so many boyfriends. Now that you're waiting tables on the Downtown Mall. Guys will flock to you.

HANNAH: I don't think so.

TRISH: Plus, the darkness.

HANNAH: What darkness?

TRISH: The darkness of cancer.

HANNAH: That makes me feel strange.

TRISH: But you know what I mean. I know you do. When my dad got sick, it was like I produced some special pheromone. Guys just looked at me differently. They looked at me all the time. Like they wanted to gobble me up. It'll happen to you, too.

HANNAH: One time, maybe five years ago, I had this sudden desperate hope that Pops would get sick, because if Pops got sick, Stephen Strange couldn't break up with me. I've never said that out loud to anyone. But I've been thinking about it a lot. Ever since Pops was diagnosed this summer. And I've been feeling guilty a lot. I broke up with Stephen Strange, and a few months later, Pops was diagnosed.

TRISH: What else have you never said out loud?

HANNAH: I'm scared of the dark.

TRISH: You talk about that all the time.

HANNAH: I'm deathly afraid of anal sex.

TRISH: Me too.

HANNAH: Ha. I wish I were prettier.

TRISH: Everyone wishes they were prettier.

HANNAH: I think about my body all day long.

TRISH: Think about it how?

HANNAH: I wish I were skinnier.

TRISH: So does everyone.

HANNAH: There's this thing I sometimes do during workshop, under the table so no one can see, where I measure my thighs with my hands.

TRISH: Show me?

HANNAH: Like this.

TRISH: How do you know where to put your hands so that it's the same measurement every time?

HANNAH: I love that you asked that.

TRISH: Show me.

HANNAH: See these two moles?

TRISH: Yeah.

HANNAH: If I can't get both my hands around my thigh and make the thumbs touch between these two moles, then I'm heavier than I want to be.

TRISH: Have you ever been able to close your hands above this top mole right here.

HANNAH: Once. For a little while. But I was younger. I used to be a size zero.

TRISH: Me too.

HANNAH: Now I'm a size eight.

TRISH: God, that's brave.

HANNAH: What is?

TRISH: Saying your size aloud.

HANNAH: It's just a size.

TRISH: But admitting it.

HANNAH: One time a nurse took my weight and then told me I hid it well. That's what she said: 'Wow, you hide it well.' I told the doctor, and the doctor was horrified. Now I don't get my weight taken anymore. It's written in my charts: *Do not weigh this woman.*

TRISH: You're leaving something out.

HANNAH: Like what?

TRISH: A detail. My father was a doctor. You're leaving something out.

HANNAH: I used to not eat as much as I should. I called myself a vegetarian, but really I just didn't eat. There were whole days when I'd only eat a boiled onion and a handful of rice cakes.

TRISH: How skinny did you get?

HANNAH: *Skinny* skinny. I looked sick.

TRISH: But you probably looked good in jeans. Were you ever hospitalized?

HANNAH: No, no. It never got that bad. I totally looked down on girls who got that bad. This one girl at boarding school, she read aloud an essay in class once about using a Magic Marker to make herself throw up, and I remember feeling so sorry for her because . . .

TRISH: Because what?

HANNAH: Nothing. I just thought she was pathetic, which I know now is pathetic in itself.

TRISH: But you thought the marker was pathetic.

HANNAH: I don't know.

TRISH: Because you didn't need to use a marker.

HANNAH: I don't know what you mean.

TRISH: To gag yourself. That's what you're leaving out. You could just use your finger.

HANNAH: I told you. I just didn't eat.

TRISH: But sometimes you vomited.

HANNAH: Once or twice.

TRISH: Sometimes still you vomit.

HANNAH: Why do you say that?

TRISH: Just say it. Say it out loud. It'll be something else you've never admitted. But then you will have. Say it to me and then you'll be able to move on.

HANNAH: I told Stephen Strange. I said it out loud to him. When we were breaking up. I told him I'd been vomiting the whole six years.

TRISH: What did he say?

HANNAH: It's too excruciating.

TRISH: Tell me.

HANNAH: We were in the car. He was driving. We were going over the Bay Bridge. I'd just gotten back from that writing seminar in Russia, and he picked me up at the airport and drove me to the Eastern Shore so we could say hi to my mom and Pops. Pops had lost so much weight. We were all so excited for him. We hadn't noticed the yellow in his eyes, and he hadn't told anyone about the lower back pain. So it was mostly just this celebration of how thin he looked and how I was home from Russia safely. Every time Stephen tried to touch me,

I found a reason to move away from him. When we got in his car to drive back to Charlottesville, I started crying like I was homesick for my parents, like I was some fourth-grade girl or something. He knew something was wrong. I couldn't believe I was about to be trapped with him for three hours.

TRISH: Did you break up with him in the car?

HANNAH: It was the longest drive of my life. I told him I was bulimic, that I'd been hiding it from him the whole time. I was trying to make him hate me. I was trying to show him how wrong we were for each other.

TRISH: But that didn't work.

HANNAH: No. It didn't.

TRISH: Tell me what he said.

HANNAH: He got turned on.

TRISH: No!

HANNAH: He put his hand on his crotch and pushed down on himself like he was in real pain. He told me he had an erection. I was so stunned I couldn't speak. My cheeks turned bright red.

TRISH: They're bright red now.

HANNAH: He told me he was turned on because I'd finally opened up to him. He said he knew I kept secrets, but he didn't know what kind. He said that my revelation made him feel extraordinarily close to me. And I . . . I just . . .

TRISH: Tell me.

HANNAH: I wanted to vomit. But for real. Two people in a car never had more opposite but concurrent experiences.

TRISH: You're so brave.

HANNAH: I don't know what you mean by that.

TRISH: You will. One day you will.

WINTER 2005—
PATRICK CALLS HANNAH FOR THE FIRST TIME

Hannah is in her tiny apartment on High Street. Her stepfather is in hospice. In Charlottesville, she drinks and waits tables and writes silly stories about silly versions of herself doing silly things. She is quiet, and she is angry. When the phone rings, she is standing at her window. She is looking at the sky. She is thinking she would like to punch someone.

PATRICK: Is this Hannah?

HANNAH: Who's this?

PATRICK: This is Patrick. I'm a friend of Trish and George's. You know Trish and George?

HANNAH: I know who you are. We've met.

PATRICK: Trish gave me your number.

HANNAH: Okay.

PATRICK: You play Scrabble?

HANNAH: I do.

PATRICK: Are you any good?

HANNAH: My family won't play with me since I learned the two-letter words. They say I'm not fun anymore.

PATRICK: You play by the rules?

HANNAH: I use the word list, not the dictionary.

PATRICK: Terrific. Meet me in ten?

HANNAH: Come again?

PATRICK: To play Scrabble.

HANNAH: Where are you?

PATRICK: Coffee shop. Downtown Mall. Trish says you live nearby.

HANNAH: I do.

PATRICK: A person can get anywhere in Charlottesville in ten minutes.

HANNAH: Don't you have a girlfriend?

PATRICK: Holly doesn't play Scrabble.

HANNAH: So this isn't a date.

PATRICK: Absolutely not.

HANNAH: Do you know about my stepfather? We call him Pops.

PATRICK: Trish told me. Do you know about my grandfather?

HANNAH: He was an endowed professor.

PATRICK: He shot himself.

HANNAH: Pops is dying. Sometimes I cry. In public. Without warning. It's gross.

PATRICK: I promise not to take it easy on you.

HANNAH: That's funny.

PATRICK: Are you busy?

HANNAH: Not really.

PATRICK: See you in ten.

FEBRUARY 2014—
NINE YEARS LATER, HANNAH & PATRICK
DISCUSS HAVING CHILDREN

It's early afternoon. They've slept through breakfast and brunch. There's no food in their fridge. The only place that's still serving lunch at 2:00 p.m. is a little Thai café just down the block from their apartment.

HANNAH: I've never been this hungover.

PATRICK: Order something spicy. It'll help.

HANNAH: Jesus. We can't keep doing this to ourselves. Chicago is killing us.

PATRICK: Why not?

HANNAH: Money, for one. We're getting older, for two. I'm scared about my liver. Sometimes it hurts. It hurts now. Can I drink your water? The waitress will bring you more.

PATRICK: I know what would help.

HANNAH: Don't say alcohol. Hair of the dog doesn't work for me. I'll be sick. If I get another tenure-track offer, I think we shouldn't turn it down again. I think we should move.

PATRICK: Will you tell the waitress what you want?

HANNAH: I'll have the Szechwan vegetables, extra spicy. Thank you. May we have more water?

PATRICK: I'll have the pad Thai.

HANNAH: Thank you.

PATRICK: I don't mean hair of the dog. I don't mean help you *now*. I mean help us in general.

HANNAH: I don't want to stop drinking. I'd rather get it under control.

PATRICK: A baby.

HANNAH: We've talked about this.

PATRICK: Actually, we haven't talked about it. You said you didn't want children, and that was that.

HANNAH: You married a woman who said she didn't want children. That seems like the extent of the conversation to me.

PATRICK: I think we'd be good at it.

HANNAH: It's two p.m. We're eating our first meal of the day. I'm shivering. I'm literally shivering. My liver is shivering. It's shuddering. I can feel it thudding, like a heartbeat. Look at my hand. That's palsy. And look at you. Your eyes are yellow. They look like Pops's eyes right before he died. And he was stage four-B. What makes you think we'd be good at it? We'd kill it. We can barely walk the dog.

PATRICK: I love Elmer.

HANNAH: I love Elmer, too. You walk him twice a week. I walk him all the time.

PATRICK: So this is about me now? This is about how useless I am?

HANNAH: I'm just saying, you're not the most responsible.

PATRICK: You're saying that if you were married to a man who was more responsible, you'd want kids? Do you know how offensive that is? That hurts my feelings.

HANNAH: You're putting words in my mouth. I don't want children. With anyone.

PATRICK: Then why do you do that?

HANNAH: Do what?

PATRICK: Stare at them with a dopey smile on your face. You're doing it now. You're looking out the window and you're smiling like a dope at that baby on that man's shoulders.

HANNAH: I smile because otherwise I'll scowl. I've trained myself. It's years of hard work.

PATRICK: Like you trained yourself to laugh instead of cry when your brother and sister ganged up on you when you were little.

HANNAH: Yes! Just like that.

PATRICK: And I've never believed that either.

HANNAH: You're being unkind.

PATRICK: I'm bored.

HANNAH: Only boring people are bored.

PATRICK: I hate that.

HANNAH: I know. Thank you. This looks good.

PATRICK: Thank you.

HANNAH: Do you have spicy mustard? And maybe a side of chili oil?

PATRICK: Can't you just eat it as it comes? You've ruined your taste buds. You might as well be eating Alpo.

HANNAH: Can we agree to eat in silence?

PATRICK: —

HANNAH: Can we?

PATRICK: —

HANNAH: Hello?

PATRICK: I thought you wanted silence.

HANNAH: No babies.

JUNE 2006—
TRISH TEXTS HANNAH

Hannah is at her parents' house on the Eastern Shore of Maryland. Earlier this morning, when she walked in for her brunch shift, the floor manager told her to go straight home. "He's going to die today," her manager said. "Your sister called, and she told me to say that. Also, I think your phone's dead." Her phone was dead. It had died while she was out the night before. She'd gotten so drunk that she'd forgotten to charge it. She'd also gotten so drunk that she'd made out with a guy who waits tables with Trish, and who also happens to have been a student in a class Hannah taught as a grad student the year before. They didn't have sex, and Hannah is so glad they didn't have sex. But none of that matters anymore, because it's the next night now, and Pops is dead. The undertaker has come and gone. Alone in her bedroom, Hannah checks her phone for the first time since it's charged. There are a dozen missed texts. They are all from Trish.

TRISH: You made out with Josh?

TRISH: Are you a fucking perv?

TRISH: He's barely 22.

TRISH: You're like eight years older than he is.

TRISH: He's a fucking kid.

TRISH: What kind of piece of trash are you?

TRISH: You disgust me.

TRISH: He was your student.

TRISH: Last year he was IN YOUR CLASS.

TRISH: He's a baby. He's a senior IN COLLEGE.

TRISH: I'm so gnarled out right now.

TRISH: You're sick.

TRISH: Anything? Anything at all to say?

FALL 2006—
HANNAH WAITS TABLES AT A DOWNTOWN
STEAKHOUSE IN CHARLOTTESVILLE

It's past closing time, but there's a table of men in Hannah's section who haven't settled up. Policy says you don't deliver a bill until a table asks for it. There's still wine in their glasses, and policy also says never to be rude. Hannah makes a pass through the dining room, and one of the men flags her over. Pops has been dead for only a few months.

MAN: Excuse me? Hey. It's Hannah, right?

HANNAH: Yes, sir.

MAN: Can you help us with something?

HANNAH: Sure.

MAN: It's a tradition.

HANNAH: Okay.

MAN: We do this every year.

HANNAH: How can I help?

MAN: We need you to pick a credit card.

HANNAH: Sir?

MAN: We put our cards in this napkin. See? We need you to pick which of us has to pay.

HANNAH: —

MAN: Just stick your hand in and choose. It's tradition.

HANNAH: I'd prefer not to.

MAN: Here you go. Just pick. Whichever one you like. Won't bite.

HANNAH: Come on, man.

MAN: Pick a good one.

HANNAH: I don't—

MAN: Reach right in and choose.

HANNAH: But I—

MAN: Be smart about it.

HANNAH: Sir, I—

MAN: That's the man who's going to put the tip in.

HANNAH: —

MAN: Do you get it?

HANNAH: I . . .

MAN: The tip. He's gonna put just the tip in.

HANNAH: Yeah. I get it.

MAN: Pick a card.

HANNAH: That one.

MAN: The top one?

HANNAH: Sure.

MAN: The top one it is.

HANNAH: Can I bring the bill now?

MAN: Only if you want the tip.

HALLOWEEN 2006— HANNAH TENDS BAR, HOLLY & PATRICK ORDER A DRINK, TRISH WALKS BY

Next door to the steakhouse is a French bistro known for its meat loaf, where Hannah also waits tables. But tonight the place is slammed, and the manager asks her to cover the bar. She texts Patrick, and he shows up with Holly, who's already drunk. Maybe they're both already drunk. Hannah pours them bourbons anyway. While they're talking, Trish—in cut-offs and covered in mud—passes slowly by the restaurant, her arms dead at her sides.

HOLLY: She takes Halloween really seriously, huh?

PATRICK: She's from Morgantown, West Virginia.

HOLLY: What's that mean?

PATRICK: They take Halloween really seriously over there.

HOLLY: Is she supposed to be a zombie or something? Is that why she's walking so slow?

PATRICK: I think she looks good.

HOLLY: Aren't you two like best friends or something?

HANNAH: We're not best friends.

HOLLY: Are y'all fighting, then?

HANNAH: We're not in middle school.

HOLLY: But there's something going on between you two, right? You're mad at each other?

HANNAH: We're just taking a minute.

PATRICK: Are you coming to our show later?

HANNAH: I'm closing tonight.

PATRICK: The show doesn't start until ten. There's a party after. At our place. Come by whenever.

HANNAH: House parties aren't really my scene.

HOLLY: What *is* your scene?

HANNAH: I don't have a scene. Can you keep it down a little? This isn't actually a bar. It's more of a restaurant, you know?

HOLLY: You like playing Scrabble with other people's boyfriends. Is that your scene?

HANNAH: What? I don't . . . What?

PATRICK: She's pretending to be jealous. Ignore her.

HOLLY: I'm not pretending anything.

PATRICK: She's drunk. Ignore her.

HOLLY: I'm not drunk.

PATRICK: You should come to the show.

HANNAH: Will Trish be there?

PATRICK: So you two *are* fighting.

HANNAH: I just don't want to get into a big thing with her tonight. She can be intense, you know?

HOLLY: I know how she can be.

PATRICK: I just want all my girls to get along.

HOLLY: *I'm* your girl. She's not your girl. Neither of them is your girl.

HANNAH: I'm not his girl. I know that. I promise. I'm not anyone's girl.

HOLLY: I do not like that person. I do not like Trish.

PATRICK: Everyone just needs to calm down.

HANNAH: Maybe you can settle up? It's getting kind of loud. And my manager keeps looking over here.

HOLLY: What's she going to do? Kick us out?

HANNAH: Patrick? Can you—?

PATRICK: Okay. Okay. Everyone's happy. Everyone's fine. Here. Here's a twenty. Is twenty enough?

HOLLY: Twenty fucking dollars? For that pour?

HANNAH: Can you, please? Can you get her out of here? I'm sorry. But this is my job and I . . .

JULY 2016—
A TEXT EXCHANGE BETWEEN HANNAH, PATRICK, & TRISH

Hannah is alone in a changing room inside the Zara on Fifth Avenue. She's called her sister and brother. She's called her mother. There are still hours for her to pass alone before her book launch. She has stripped down to her bra and underpants and is now sitting on the tiny bench of the dressing room, a stack of clothes beside her. She doesn't have the energy to try anything, but she also doesn't have the energy to put her own clothes back on.

HANNAH: Hate to interrupt. This will be my only text to the two of you. But did you ever have sex before last week? I need to know if I should get tested for STDs.

PATRICK: No. We didn't.

HANNAH: Thank you.

TRISH: We didn't plan this.

TRISH: I promise.

TRISH: This only just started.

TRISH: We never realized what good friends we were.

TRISH: We aren't trying to hurt you.

TRISH: You have to understand.

PATRICK: Trish—STOP TEXTING.

MAY 2012—
HANNAH & PATRICK IN THEIR APARTMENT ABOVE
A POTBELLY IN CHICAGO

Sober and in bed at 10:00 p.m.

PATRICK: That was good sex.

HANNAH: Very good sex.

PATRICK: I'm so happy.

HANNAH: So, so happy.

PATRICK: Do you feel lucky?

HANNAH: I do.

PATRICK: What's your favorite part about being together?

HANNAH: I can tell you anything.

PATRICK: Same.

HANNAH: And you look good with your shirt tucked into your pants.

PATRICK: I look better clothed than naked.

HANNAH: You wear clothes well.

PATRICK: You look better naked.

HANNAH: Said every man to every woman ever.

FEBRUARY 2013—
HANNAH & PATRICK VISIT MORGANTOWN, WEST VIRGINIA

A hotel in West Virginia. Midday. They're fully clothed and lying on top of the covers of the queen-size bed.

HANNAH: But it's a tenure-track job.

PATRICK: The grocery store here is a Piggly Wiggly.

HANNAH: I grew up with Piggly Wigglys.

PATRICK: No. You grew up in the South, where Piggly Wigglys existed. Your family didn't actually shop at them.

HANNAH: You don't know.

PATRICK: Did your family shop at the Piggly Wiggly?

HANNAH: They shopped at the A&P, but I'm not sure there's a palpable distinction.

PATRICK: What's your first memory?

HANNAH: Of grocery stores? Or in general?

PATRICK: Of driving into this town today. What's the first thing you think of when you think of Morgantown?

HANNAH: Honestly? I think of Trish, because this is where her parents taught. This is where she grew up. It explains a lot.

PATRICK: Are you trying to be funny?

HANNAH: I just mean, she's a really good storyteller, right? Her stories are factually very good even if she's erratic and unreliable and doesn't try to publish them anymore. But her grammar has always been suspect. In workshop, we'd kind of marvel at what she did and didn't know about the English language.

PATRICK: What a bunch of snobs. Maybe they were typos.

HANNAH: I'm being called a snob by the man who told me not to drink water from the faucet at this hotel?

PATRICK: It's a motel.

HANNAH: Your inconsistency when it comes to Trish and George is completely annoying. You can call her indiscriminate. You can say her stories are dumb. But when I want to talk about the discrepancy between her instinctive ability as an artist and her parochial linguistic tendencies, you shoot me down.

PATRICK: I don't give a fuck how you talk about Trish and George. I don't give a fuck if we ever see them again.

HANNAH: Can we change the subject? Or at least return to the subject at hand? Are we really considering turning this job down? I've been on the market three years. This is my first tenure-track offer.

PATRICK: We live in Chicago! We have the world's best apartment!

HANNAH: We can barely afford to live in it.

PATRICK: So we'll cut back. If we cut back, then we can afford it. We can.

HANNAH: The only reason we can pay the rent now is because my mom is subsidizing us. And we can't cut back. We literally can't. We say that every month and nothing changes. We have zero savings.

PATRICK: Why do we need savings?

HANNAH: Do you know you've never been happy with where we are until there's a threat we're about to leave?

PATRICK: I love Chicago. I've always loved Chicago.

HANNAH: Wrong. When you got to Chicago, all you talked about was how much you missed Charlottesville. You complain all the time that no good bands ever come through.

PATRICK: I didn't miss Charlottesville. I missed not being there to open a restaurant with my parents.

HANNAH: You refuse to live in the present! You refuse to appreciate what you have!

PATRICK: I refuse to settle.

HANNAH: Why does contentment have to equal settling?

PATRICK: Did you have an answer earlier, when you thought I was asking about your earliest memory in general?

HANNAH: I did.

PATRICK: I have a first memory, too. It's being on the boat with my mom and dad, being in the hammock, watching my dad skin a fish. I learned how to cook because of them. It's why I wanted to be there when they finally opened their place.

HANNAH: Is the boat a happy memory?

PATRICK: One of my happiest.

HANNAH: That's quite sweet. Thanks for sharing it with me.

PATRICK: Of course.

HANNAH: Do you want to know mine?

PATRICK: Your what?

HANNAH: My earliest memory?

PATRICK: We should probably figure out what we're doing here. We should explore the town, right? Find some pizza? Maybe a bar? Look—watch this: I'm drinking water from the tap. I'm drinking all the water. I can change. I don't have to be a snob. You want me to change, I can change. We can cut back at home. I can stay in budget. Maybe we should call George and Trish? See what they think? Maybe they'd drive down and meet us. She could show us the town. It's just a thought.

JUNE 2012—
THE DAY AFTER PATRICK PROPOSES, HANNAH
CALLS HER MOTHER

It's one hundred degrees, the month's high in Chicago. Hannah is watching Elmer crazy-eight in and out of the water along the beach-line at the Edgewater dog park. She is alone. The sixth anniversary of Pops's death is one week away.

HANNAH: I have news.

MOTHER: *I* have news.

HANNAH: Oh. Okay. What news?

MOTHER: I'm getting a divorce.

HANNAH: —

MOTHER: I've had enough.

HANNAH: You're not doing this again.

MOTHER: That's right. Because this time I'm divorcing for real.

HANNAH: You do everything so quickly.

MOTHER: Don't be a scold.

HANNAH: You hate being alone.

MOTHER: I love being alone.

HANNAH: After Pops died, you couldn't go to the grocery store without company. Patrick and I had to take you. Do you remember?

MOTHER: You told me not to get remarried. I didn't listen to you. I'm listening now.

HANNAH: I told you not to get remarried because you'd only known him five months and because Pops had died just the year before.

MOTHER: I'll go mad.

HANNAH: Are you taking your medications?

MOTHER: I'm not depressed.

HANNAH: But are you taking them?

MOTHER: You stopped taking Prozac. Why do I have to keep taking medication if you don't? I'm not a depressed person. Fragile people need pills, and I am not a fragile person. I'm an angry person. I'm a rageful person full of ire. Is there a pill for that?

HANNAH: Does your doctor know?

MOTHER: I don't need his permission.

HANNAH: There are all kinds of side effects when you go cold turkey. You know this.

MOTHER: Damn it.

HANNAH: Don't be mad.

MOTHER: You called me, didn't you? What's your news already?

HANNAH: Please, don't be mad at me.

MOTHER: I'm not mad at you. I'm fucking livid at life, and you're not listening to what I'm saying, so tell me your goddamn news.

HANNAH: It's not important.

JUNE 2012—
TWO MINUTES LATER, HANNAH CALLS HER
FATHER

Elmer is still crazy-eighting. Hannah can feel all one hundred degrees, streaming like stinging ants up and down her arms, in and around the elastic of her underwear, along her upper lip, down her lower back, between her inner thighs . . .

HANNAH: Guess what?

FATHER: Hey, kid. I've got a question for you.

HANNAH: I have news.

FATHER: What are you doing August tenth?

HANNAH: August tenth?

FATHER: Can you make it to Asheville for the weekend?

HANNAH: I'm usually getting ready to teach that time of year.

FATHER: But do you think you can make it?

HANNAH: I'm not sure. I'd need to talk to—

FATHER: Invite your roommate. It's gonna be a party.

HANNAH: His name is Patrick.

FATHER: You, Patrick, whatever. We're inviting everyone. CeCe and I are renewing our vows.

HANNAH: —

FATHER: Ten years!

HANNAH: —

FATHER: Hot diggity! Can you believe it?

HANNAH: I can't believe it. No. I really can't believe it.

FATHER: I knew I'd surprise you! Gonna be the party of the decade.

JUNE 2012—
ONE MINUTE LATER, HANNAH CALLS HER SISTER

Elmer is wet and happy and exhausted and has just now collapsed at Hannah's feet, which are covered in sand and wet dog hair. She pours water into his mouth while she waits for her sister to answer.

HANNAH: Speechless.

GRETA: What's up?

HANNAH: Utterly speechless. Hushed. Agog. Dumbstruck. Wordless.

GRETA: I don't think 'agog' means what you think it means.

HANNAH: Agape, dumbfounded, whatever. I have news.

GRETA: Did you sell a book?

HANNAH: Your mother—

GRETA: *Your* mother.

HANNAH: Your mother thinks she's getting a divorce.

GRETA: Not again.

HANNAH: It gets better.

GRETA: Do you have to tell me? Maybe you don't need to tell me.

HANNAH: Your father is renewing his vows.

GRETA: Shoot a turkey.

HANNAH: Back-to-back phone calls. You can't make this up, is what I'm saying.

GRETA: You're having quite a day.

HANNAH: But guess what?

GRETA: There's more?

HANNAH: Patrick and I are getting married.

GRETA: —

MARCH 2013—
PATRICK COMES HOME FROM WHOLE FOODS

Hannah is grading papers at the kitchen table. Elmer is asleep on the floor beside her, his soft cheek pressed against her foot. If she moves, he wakes up and moves with her.

HANNAH: Thanks for going to the store.

PATRICK: You know how I feel about shopping for groceries.

HANNAH: I've never met a man who could spend so many hours in a grocery store and not get bored.

PATRICK: You can come with me whenever you want.

HANNAH: It reminds me too much of Pops, of feeling kidnapped whenever he and Mom would take me to run errands and we'd end up gone for hours instead of thirty minutes.

PATRICK: I'm your kidnapper now?

HANNAH: Kiss me.

PATRICK: Where?

HANNAH: Here. On the cheek. My favorite kidnapper. What's this?

PATRICK: Lamb.

HANNAH: You bought lamb?

PATRICK: Lamb chops.

HANNAH: You know I don't . . . Never mind. This says fifty-seven dollars. Were they on sale?

PATRICK: You're going to love them.

HANNAH: But were they on sale?

PATRICK: I don't know. They were fifty-seven dollars. On sale or not on sale, that's how much they were.

HANNAH: Why are you acting like this?

PATRICK: Like what?

HANNAH: Like you don't understand what a big deal this is.

PATRICK: How big a deal is this?

HANNAH: We have one hundred dollars for the week.

PATRICK: I didn't spend it all.

HANNAH: But . . .

PATRICK: We still have twenty dollars.

HANNAH: This is one bag of groceries. This is—Jesus. There's nothing else in here but carrots and an onion. That's our money for the week.

PATRICK: We can use the credit card.

HANNAH: No. We can't.

PATRICK: Yes. We can.

HANNAH: But that's what you always say, and then we don't pay it off, and then we always spend more. You promised. You said you'd stay in budget.

PATRICK: We can skip going out tonight.

HANNAH: We aren't going out tonight. We can't. You spent all our money.

PATRICK: —

HANNAH: What? What's that look supposed to mean?

PATRICK: Now you've ruined it.

HANNAH: Ruined what?

PATRICK: I don't even feel like cooking anymore.

JULY 2013—
HANNAH TELLS TRISH A SECRET

They're walking around Chicago, pretending to shop for trinkets until it's an appropriate time to start drinking. It's late afternoon. They are sunburned and thirsty. The breeze off the lake is sandy and divine.

HANNAH: You know how women keep secrets?

TRISH: I know that you keep secrets.

HANNAH: You keep secrets, too.

TRISH: I'm more of a liar. I'm not a professional secret-keeper like you.

HANNAH: Are you calling me repressed?

TRISH: That's an interesting leap. Do you think you're repressed?

HANNAH: I had a boyfriend once who asked if I'd ever been messed with. That's how he put it—'Have you ever been messed with?' Isn't that a weird thing to ask a person?

TRISH: Had you been messed with?

HANNAH: No. I don't think so. But I spent a lot of time after that trying to remember whether or not I had been.

TRISH: Just him asking that messed with you.

HANNAH: Probably. Yes. Those are cute earrings.

TRISH: Would you wear them?

HANNAH: Me? No. They're too dangly.

TRISH: You don't actually think they're cute, then.

HANNAH: I think other women besides me keep secrets.

TRISH: Of course they do. But you specialize in it.

HANNAH: Remember when you and I took a break from being friends?

TRISH: You missed my wedding.

HANNAH: This was another time, a couple years later, right after I sold my first book and bought the MINI.

TRISH: And?

HANNAH: Patrick and I went to New Orleans. We drove the MINI. It was supposed to be a celebration.

TRISH: I knew about that. We weren't not friends. We were just taking some time apart, seeing less of each other.

HANNAH: Sure. However you want to put it.

TRISH: What happened? Did something happen down there? Did he cheat on you? Did you cheat on him?

HANNAH: A man thought I was a prostitute.

TRISH: What man?

HANNAH: A man at a bar.

TRISH: What were you wearing?

HANNAH: Cowboy boots. A black dress. I wasn't wearing a bra, but only because you couldn't wear a bra with that dress. In retrospect, it was a regrettable outfit.

TRISH: What kind of bar?

HANNAH: It's embarrassing.

TRISH: Where was Patrick?

HANNAH: That's what's embarrassing.

TRISH: Was it a strip club?

HANNAH: I can't go in those places. They make me hate my body, and they make me angry at men. It wasn't a strip club.

TRISH: What was it then?

HANNAH: It was Harrah's.

TRISH: The casino?

HANNAH: Yes.

TRISH: Ah. I see.

HANNAH: Do you?

TRISH: Patrick was playing poker.

HANNAH: Yes.

TRISH: And you were alone at the bar.

HANNAH: Yes. I'd been alone all day. I was lonely. I was bored. I wanted to be with him.

TRISH: So you got dressed up.

HANNAH: Yes. And I went to the bar where the serious poker gets played. It's separated from the blackjack tables and stuff. Like, it's special. Patrick saw me and I saw him, and I ordered a gin and tonic, and I just sat there like an idiot.

TRISH: Did you have a book?

HANNAH: I was reading something or other.

TRISH: And a man walked up.

HANNAH: A man who'd been sitting at Patrick's table.

TRISH: And he asked if you were a prostitute.

HANNAH: He asked if I wanted to sit with him. To bring him luck. He said he'd take me out after, make it worth my time.

TRISH: What did you say?

HANNAH: Honestly? I don't even remember. My chest got all blotchy.

TRISH: It's charming the way you wear your feelings on your skin.

HANNAH: I was heartbroken. I hadn't realized you could have guests at the table. I hadn't known that was an option. Patrick could have had me sit with him. He could have invited me. But he didn't.

TRISH: You would never have told me this before you were married.

HANNAH: I know. You're right. I wouldn't have felt safe telling you.

TRISH: But now you feel safe.

HANNAH: I do. But that's not even the secret.

TRISH: What's the secret?

HANNAH: How much money he lost during those two weeks. Every day, he went to those tables. Every day.

TRISH: How much?

HANNAH: It wasn't even his. It was mine. From the book. And I still had so much debt, so much credit card debt. I didn't pay my debt, but I did give him money.

TRISH: Enough money to have paid your debts?

HANNAH: All of it. Yes.

TRISH: That's a lot of money.

HANNAH: It wasn't his fault. It was mine because I let him.

TRISH: What did you think would have happened if you hadn't given it to him?

HANNAH: We'd have broken up. Or he'd have gotten mad.

TRISH: He would have pouted.

HANNAH: Yes. He would have pouted.

TRISH: And you'd have given in eventually.

HANNAH: Yes.

TRISH: Was that the only time?

HANNAH: Is it ever the only time?

TRISH: Exactly.

MARCH 2013—
HANNAH CALLS HER SISTER

For privacy, Hannah takes Elmer for a walk. Lately, it feels like she is taking more and more walks, that there is more and more need for privacy. She and Patrick have been married only three months.

HANNAH: Do you think I'm a good listener?

GRETA: I think you're very observant.

HANNAH: Are you observant?

GRETA: Everyone in this family is.

HANNAH: Is that code for something? Is that our way of acknowledging how judgmental we are?

GRETA: You're thinking of something specific, but you're speaking in abstractions. If you'd just speak in specifics, I could offer better advice.

HANNAH: I don't think I'm calling for advice.

GRETA: What's on your mind, then?

HANNAH: Do you like blue cheese dressing?

GRETA: No one in our family likes blue cheese dressing. You know that. Is that why you're calling? This is strange.

HANNAH: What about lamb?

GRETA: Mutton?

HANNAH: No. Fresh spring lamb. How do you feel about lamb?

GRETA: We don't eat lamb.

HANNAH: Right. I know that.

GRETA: Remember the lamb babies on the farm when we were little, before the divorce? They were so cute. And they all had names. They were our pets. I miss those little guys. Those little lamb babies.

HANNAH: We each had one. We each had a baby lamb. God, I seriously had no idea how privileged we were.

GRETA: Have you started eating lamb?

HANNAH: Maybe I'm being unreasonable. I can't tell.

GRETA: What happened?

HANNAH: Do you think it's strange that Patrick doesn't know I don't eat lamb?

GRETA: —

HANNAH: Hello?

GRETA: Oh.

HANNAH: Oh, what?

GRETA: I get it now.

HANNAH: Get what?

GRETA: You know I love Patrick, right? You know that?

HANNAH: But what?

GRETA: He *does* know you don't eat lamb.

HANNAH: Then why would he buy it?

GRETA: Because he doesn't . . .

HANNAH: Just say it. I won't be mad.

GRETA: He doesn't think about things.

HANNAH: He doesn't think about things?

GRETA: He doesn't think about people things.

HANNAH: What do you mean? Now *you're* speaking in abstractions.

GRETA: He doesn't think about you.

HANNAH: I'm hanging up.

GRETA: You said you wouldn't get mad.

HANNAH: I'm not mad. I'm unhappy. I want to hang up before I start crying.

GRETA: I'm sorry. Do you want to change the subject?

FALL 2006—
SEVEN YEARS EARLIER, HANNAH REVISITS THE GRIEF COUSELOR

From here, Hannah will walk straight to her lunch shift. She's thinking how funny it is that she's wearing all black to talk to a grief counselor. She's thinking the grief counselor is an idiot who assumes her outfit is an outward expression of her intense inner sorrow. She feels sorry for the counselor and how stupid she is. She feels sorry for everybody and how stupid they are. Years later—nearly a decade and a half from now—she will wonder what might have happened if she'd privileged earnestness and honesty over irony and indifference just once.

COUNSELOR: How's the Prozac?

HANNAH: I'm sleeping a lot.

COUNSELOR: That's good. That's good.

HANNAH: I'm sleeping all the time.

COUNSELOR: Say more.

HANNAH: I'm sleeping during the day.

COUNSELOR: Napping.

HANNAH: Under the table, usually during meals.

COUNSELOR: Explain?

HANNAH: I go home on the weekends to be with my mom.

COUNSELOR: Yes.

HANNAH: My sister comes home. My brother brings his family. We keep my mom company.

COUNSELOR: And that's when you're sleeping?

HANNAH: While they're eating lunch, I'm under the table. I hadn't been aware I was doing it. But my sister took a picture of me.

COUNSELOR: And you were under the table?

HANNAH: I was under the table, and I was asleep. My head was on the floor. The floor is tile. There's not a rug. There is no carpet. They were sitting at the table eating. It looked like they were having fun. It looked like they were making a lot of noise. And there I was with my head on the tile, fast asleep.

COUNSELOR: You think it's the Prozac?

HANNAH: I think I'm sleeping right now.

JANUARY 2007—
HANNAH CALLS HER SISTER

Hannah is sitting on top of a washing machine, waiting for her clothes to dry. She's dressed in black. It feels like she's always dressed in black or starched white, depending on the restaurant. It feels like she's always working or about to be working, and she always smells like meat loaf—sometimes steak—again, depending on the restaurant.

GRETA: She did not say that.

HANNAH: She did. This weird old woman walked up to me while I was waiting for the trolley and said, 'You look like the kind of girl a man wants to hurt.'

GRETA: Perhaps you're exaggerating for effect?

HANNAH: And then she talked about her daughter, and she asked me if I had a daughter, and then she wanted to know if I knew about the rapist in town . . . What does the kind of girl a man wants to hurt even look like?

GRETA: Like you, I guess.

HANNAH: I wish I had a boyfriend.

GRETA: Because he'd protect you?

HANNAH: Don't be mean. I wish Patrick were my boyfriend.

GRETA: Doesn't he have a girlfriend?

HANNAH: They broke up.

GRETA: Didn't he have brain surgery?

HANNAH: Does brain surgery mean I can't have a crush?

GRETA: I think you're bored. I don't actually think you have a crush on him. Maybe it's good for you to be on your own. You were with Stephen Strange for six years and you were miserable the whole time.

HANNAH: I liked him the first year. I loved him. Adored him. Worshipped him!

GRETA: Then spent the next five years wanting to break up with him and not knowing how.

HANNAH: That was complicated. I was a virgin. It took me a long time to get over all of Mom's warnings about men and sex and having to be in love. All those times she talked to me about notches on a belt.

GRETA: Notches on *my* belt, you mean.

HANNAH: Ha. Yes. You had all those wicked notches. And notches were obviously bad. If I had a quarter for every time she's told me that a man will have sex with anyone . . .

GRETA: Any*thing*. She got that line from Maury Povich.

HANNAH: Jerry Springer is more like it. I waited on Maury Povich last week!

GRETA: You are such a liar. Either way, she did a number on you.

HANNAH: She did a number on you, too.

GRETA: Your acne cleared up and you finally lost your baby fat and then suddenly you were like, *Oh, I'm hot, I need to ditch Stephen Strange and acquire some notches of my own.*

HANNAH: Not exactly, but sure.

GRETA: I don't want you to accuse me of sounding like Mom here, but I'm worried that until last year you'd only ever had sex with Stephen. But since moving to Charlottesville—

HANNAH: Since Pops died—

GRETA: Since Pops got sick and then died and then you started drinking and hanging out with that person from your workshop—

HANNAH: Her name is Trish, and things have been a lot better with her lately. She's been supportive.

GRETA: It just seems like you've had a lot of sex with a lot of different men. And I'm saying this to you as someone who does not believe you have to be in love to have sex. But maybe sober? And maybe with a little more intentionality?

HANNAH: Whose word is that? That's not a word you use.

GRETA: Intentionality? I use it all the time.

HANNAH: What about your intentionality?

GRETA: We're not talking about me. Does your therapist know how much sex you're having?

HANNAH: She's a grief counselor. We don't talk about things like that.

GRETA: What do you talk about?

HANNAH: I'm not actually having a lot of sex. I've had sex with seven people. And with each of those people, it's only been the once. I'm actually having very little sex when you think about it.

GRETA: That's your number? Seven?

HANNAH: What's your number?

GRETA: Men are dumb and almost all of them are the same.

HANNAH: Huh.

GRETA: I miss Pops.

HANNAH: Me too.

GRETA: It's only been six months.

HANNAH: I dream about him.

GRETA: Is he skinny and sick or fat and healthy?

HANNAH: Skinny and sick and sometimes a little creepy. Is he fat and healthy for you?

GRETA: Yep. Fat and healthy but sometimes also a little creepy.

HANNAH: Because of the pornography.

GRETA: Probably.

HANNAH: I wish he'd thought to get rid of it. But I guess when you get diagnosed with cancer, your first thought isn't necessarily to eighty-six all of your secrets to spare your family.

GRETA: That's exactly what my first thought would be. I know a woman who's so scared of her parents finding out about her sex life that she actually has a dildo buddy.

HANNAH: What's a dildo buddy?

GRETA: If either woman dies suddenly—car accident, hit-and-run, aneurism, whatever—the other one immediately removes the dildo from her bedside table.

HANNAH: I'll be your dildo buddy, and I don't even have one.

GRETA: Maybe you should get one.

MARCH 2007—
HANNAH WAKES UP IN PATRICK'S BED FOR THE FIRST TIME

It's dark. Who knows what time it is? The curtains are closed. Their stomachs are rumbling. It could be 5:00 a.m.; it could be noon.

PATRICK: What are you doing here?

HANNAH: 'I bought you. I own you.'

PATRICK: I love that movie.

HANNAH: Bill Murray's best. Andie MacDowell can't act, but I love her voice. That accent!

PATRICK: Say it again.

HANNAH: 'I bought you. I own you.'

PATRICK: What are you doing today?

HANNAH: Waiting tables. You?

PATRICK: Waiting for you to get off work.

HANNAH: Scrabble later?

PATRICK: Yes.

HANNAH: I'm oddly happy right now.

PATRICK: I wasn't expecting this.

HANNAH: It's funny, right?

PATRICK: I'm happy, too.

HANNAH: Who do you think is going to fuck it up?

PATRICK: Me.

HANNAH: Yeah. Probably.

PATRICK: I'll drink too much.

HANNAH: I'll become overly attentive.

PATRICK: I'll stay out too late and make bad choices.

HANNAH: I'll be uneasy about money and who you're talking to at bars.

PATRICK: You're my best friend. Can we agree to go back to being best friends if we mess this up?

HANNAH: I feel like we're the type of best friends who could get married, get divorced, and still be inseparable.

PATRICK: My second wife already hates you.

HANNAH: Oh my god. My second husband thinks you're worthless. He fumes when I tell him I'm going to see you.

PATRICK: And my second wife tells me I have to choose between her and you.

HANNAH: And we always choose each other.

MARCH 2007—
SEVERAL HOURS LATER, PATRICK BLOWS
HANNAH OFF

Hannah's in a starched white shirt, black slacks, shiny tie, and faded apron. Her shift at the steakhouse has already started. She should be folding napkins or polishing wineglasses or lighting tea candles. She shouldn't be answering phone calls.

PATRICK: I'm confused. Why did you cancel getting drinks with that guy? I thought you liked him. Can you hear me? You sound strange, by the way. Your throat sounds all clogged up. Are you outside? I thought you were working.

HANNAH: Doors open in five minutes. I'm in the alley, next to the dumpsters and the laundry toss. There's a breeze, that's all. There's nothing wrong with my throat.

PATRICK: It sounds like a windstorm. Can you go inside? It hurts my ears. I'm literally holding the phone away from my head.

HANNAH: We can't have our phones out in the kitchen. Chef gets angry.

PATRICK: We can talk later, then. This is annoying.

HANNAH: I'll come over when I'm off.

PATRICK: Not tonight. I have plans.

HANNAH: I thought you said you wanted to play Scrabble after my shift.

PATRICK: I think you should get drinks with that guy. What's his name? Paul?

HANNAH: His name is Pete.

PATRICK: Yeah. Pete. He seems cool.

HANNAH: —

PATRICK: Are you there?

HANNAH: I canceled drinks with Pete because of what happened last night.

PATRICK: Do you feel like you drank too much or something? You're hungover?

HANNAH: Because of what happened between *us* last night. You're being deliberately obtuse.

PATRICK: And I feel like *you're* being deliberately obtuse.

HANNAH: So last night meant nothing?

PATRICK: Last night was fun. Honestly, I'm probably the one who drank too much.

HANNAH: You never think you've drunk too much.

PATRICK: What if—what if I want you back as my best friend?

HANNAH: Meaning what?

PATRICK: What if I just want to go back to how we were and pretend last night didn't happen?

HANNAH: You said you thought you were falling in love with me.

PATRICK: Don't be such a literalist.

HANNAH: My shift is starting.

PATRICK: But why can't we just go back? Why can't we do that?

APRIL 2007—
HANNAH RUNS INTO HOLLY ON THE DOWNTOWN MALL

Holly is leaning against the exterior brick wall of the Paramount Theater. She's playing a washboard. There are bottle caps on her fingers. At her feet is a fawn-colored boxer, and beside the boxer is a box full of puppies, a squirming mass of brindles and solids. There's a handwritten sign: Pups $250 each. *When Holly sees Hannah, she stops playing.*

HOLLY: You. Hey, you. Come here.

HANNAH: I can't talk. I'm on my way to work.

HOLLY: Want a puppy?

HANNAH: You're selling them? To anyone?

HOLLY: Pick one up. They're warm.

HANNAH: Nah. Thanks, though.

HOLLY: You and Patrick are together.

HANNAH: We're friends.

HOLLY: You don't have to lie to me.

HANNAH: I'm not lying.

HOLLY: You'll end up paying for everything.

HANNAH: I don't know what you're talking about.

HOLLY: He'll use you and then dump you. We went through my inheritance in a year.

HANNAH: We're not together like that.

HOLLY: I don't get it. You're not his type.

HANNAH: Okay.

HOLLY: You're so *nice*.

HANNAH: Thanks.

HOLLY: I don't mean it as a compliment.

HANNAH: Right.

HOLLY: He puts bourbon in his coffee in the morning. You ready for that?

HANNAH: —

HOLLY: He likes wild girls. He likes girls like me. He likes a girl he can fix. He needs to be needed.

HANNAH: Got it.

HOLLY: But I got old.

HANNAH: You're not old.

HOLLY: I'm ten years older than you.

HANNAH: I guess.

HOLLY: Know what he got me for my fortieth? He got me one of those battery-operated face scrubbers. You know what I'm talking about? Did he tell you? I died laughing. He thought I could scrub a decade off my face. For my fortieth birthday, that's what he gave me. You ready for that kind of romance?

HANNAH: Like I said, I need to get to work.

MAY 2007—
HANNAH & TRISH GET A DRINK

A fancy fish place on the Downtown Mall in Charlottesville. Hannah and Trish both have on outfits.

TRISH: Let's stay alone at the bar a minute longer.

HANNAH: They found a table, though. I can see them. They're waving us over.

TRISH: It's okay. They'll still be there. You don't have to be available to Patrick all the time just because you're dating now. Distance is good.

HANNAH: I'm not available to him all the time.

TRISH: Look at them watching us. They really love us. Oh my gosh. That's so cute. You're blushing.

HANNAH: It's the gin.

TRISH: Take a sip. How's the sex?

HANNAH: Wow. Straight to that!

TRISH: Sir, excuse me? Can you watch your elbow? I'm drinking a martini with my girlfriend here, and your elbow keeps knocking into mine. Sorry, H, what were we talking about? Oh, right, sex. I don't actually like sex. Have I ever told you that? There's so much I want to tell you all of a sudden. I don't know. Now that you're with Patrick, things just feel different. You're different. Everything is how it should be. We can double-date always, and we'll be a perfect foursome. I've been waiting for this. I knew once you'd hooked up, you'd finally get together. Just because it took Patrick a minute to be convinced he was into you doesn't mean he doesn't love you already.

HANNAH: You don't like sex? With George?

TRISH: With anyone. I like making out. George is the best kisser. Sex is just . . . bleh.

HANNAH: Do you have orgasms?

TRISH: You don't have to whisper.

HANNAH: I'm not whispering. I'm just being a little quiet. This place is a lot busier than it usually is.

TRISH: Because of basketball. There's a home game.

HANNAH: Oh.

TRISH: Of course I have orgasms. Self-inflicted orgasms alone at home.

HANNAH: Huh.

TRISH: You have orgasms?

HANNAH: Yes.

TRISH: With Patrick?

HANNAH: Yes.

TRISH: Cool. Weird. I'm surprised.

HANNAH: Why are you surprised?

TRISH: You had sex with my brother, remember?

HANNAH: Meaning?

TRISH: Nothing. Nothing. Sir, excuse me, can you please not push your girlfriend's purse into my space. There's a hook under the bar. You're not supposed to put purses on bars. Ugh. Sorry, H. I don't mean to keep interrupting you. But seriously. Bar etiquette 101: no purses on bars. Am I right?

HANNAH: You're being kind of loud?

TRISH: I don't care if they hear me. I want them to hear me. I've been jabbed in the back ten times by this guy. Frankly, he should buy me a drink after how much I've spilled.

HANNAH: Did your brother tell you about the sex we had? We were both pretty drunk.

TRISH: No. No. Yuck. I don't talk to my brother about sex.

HANNAH: You guys are close.

TRISH: Does Patrick know? About my brother?

HANNAH: Are you already drunk? You're kind of acting like you do when you're drunk.

TRISH: I'm not drunk.

HANNAH: Patrick knows about your brother. I mean, it happened months ago, before we started dating, so it doesn't even matter. But, yes, I told him about it at the time. We talk about sex. We've always talked about sex.

TRISH: That'll change.

HANNAH: We should join them.

TRISH: Let's finish these drinks first. We'll spill them if we try to walk over there.

HANNAH: You're the one who taught me never to order a drink I couldn't walk away from.

TRISH: Beer. Never order a *beer* you can't walk away from. This is a martini. This is expensive. Let's finish these and then go over. Oh my god. Look at Patrick. Look at him looking at you. He looks so dumb right now. Hey! Patrick!

HANNAH: Shh.

TRISH: Hey! Patrick!

HANNAH: Put your hand down? Please?

TRISH: Patrick! Did you know that Hannah had sex with my brother?

HANNAH: What are you doing?

TRISH: Patrick! Did you know that your girlfriend had sex with my brother?

HANNAH: Why are you being like this?

TRISH: Because it's funny. Because it's fun. Stop being so glum all the time. Now I'm bored.

NOVEMBER 2009—
TWO YEARS LATER, HANNAH BUYS A MINI AFTER SELLING HER FIRST BOOK

Farmhouse: middle of nowhere, somewhere in Virginia. Sky: inky and twinkling. Elmer: asleep on leather sofa.

HANNAH: Look. My hands are shaking.

PATRICK: Yep.

HANNAH: I couldn't even drive it. I had to let my mother drive it home from the dealer. That's how nervous I was.

PATRICK: Yep.

HANNAH: Do you like it? I love it. I've always wanted a MINI. Pops used to take me to MINI conventions. I think he'd be happy.

PATRICK: Yep. You've told me that before.

HANNAH: Are you moping?

PATRICK: No.

HANNAH: But you're acting pissy. Why are you pissy?

PATRICK: You didn't ask me.

HANNAH: Ask you what?

PATRICK: You didn't even consult me.

HANNAH: About the car? It's my car.

PATRICK: —

HANNAH: For that matter, it's my money.

PATRICK: See? I knew this would happen. *My, my, my. This is mine. This is yours.* Did you think about me at all when you picked out that car? Did you think about what I do for a living?

HANNAH: What do you do for a living?

PATRICK: I'm a musician.

HANNAH: Yes?

PATRICK: I play guitar?

HANNAH: Yes?

PATRICK: I have an amp?

HANNAH: Yes?

PATRICK: You think my guitars and my amp are going to fit in that clown car when I gig?

HANNAH: I didn't think about that, but also—

PATRICK: Right. Finally. Thank you. You didn't think about me.

HANNAH: But why do they need to fit in my car? You have your own car. You don't need my car.

PATRICK: My car is a piece of shit. It's dying. There was a squirrel nest in the engine last week. An actual squirrel nest.

HANNAH: And when it dies, you'll get another car. Right?

PATRICK: With what? How am I going to afford another car? Are you going to buy it for me?

HANNAH: I don't . . . You're not asking me to buy you a car, are you? I can barely afford my bills. I'm in a debt repayment program. We're not even married.

PATRICK: This is about marriage? You want to get married?

HANNAH: I'm not saying that. Not right now anyway. We're too young.

PATRICK: You're thirty years old. You're a waitress. You're broke. But you also just sold a novel and can suddenly afford to buy yourself a brand-new MINI, but god forbid you help me buy a used piece of shit so that I can help make us money.

HANNAH: I'm at a loss for words.

PATRICK: Sounds about right.

DECEMBER 2012—
THREE YEARS LATER, THE NIGHT OF PATRICK & HANNAH'S WEDDING

It's 4:00 a.m. They're under the covers, holding hands, facing each other.

PATRICK: Why are we sober?

HANNAH: Why are we awake?

PATRICK: Want me to turn off the light?

HANNAH: Not yet. Does anything feel different?

PATRICK: No.

HANNAH: Thank god. I'd worry if it felt different. People always think it'll be different when they get married. But why would anything change? If you wanted something to change, why get married at all?

PATRICK: Your dress had pockets!

HANNAH: It's a skirt, not a dress.

PATRICK: Your skirt had pockets!

HANNAH: And you cried.

PATRICK: You handed me a tissue.

HANNAH: Because I had tissues in my pockets!

PATRICK: You looked beautiful.

HANNAH: It was a very practical outfit.

NOVEMBER 2015—
HANNAH ASKS PATRICK TO SEE A THERAPIST

They're in the kitchen. Why are they always in the kitchen when they fight? Patrick is on one side of the island. Hannah on the other. They are divided by an island. Hannah can't stop thinking about the futility of this symbolism, and she wants to pull the thought from her skull like bubblegum from the sole of a shoe.

PATRICK: I hate this town. I hate Kentucky.

HANNAH: We own a house finally. We have money in our savings account. We *have* a savings account! We have tenure-track jobs. Our dog has a yard.

PATRICK: The sidewalks are so narrow we can't even walk side by side when we take Elmer out.

HANNAH: You never take Elmer out with me anymore.

PATRICK: Because we can't walk side by side. I miss Chicago. I miss scenery. There's nothing to look at here but ugly houses.

HANNAH: We have two incomes. We can pay our bills. We have time to write.

PATRICK: Who cares if there's time to write if there's nothing to write about?

HANNAH: I have stuff to write about.

PATRICK: There you go again.

HANNAH: I just hate the idea that a person has to live in a big city in order to write. I hate that.

PATRICK: There isn't a single bartender in this town who can make a drink.

HANNAH: Andy can make a drink.

PATRICK: There isn't a single bartender in this town besides Andy who can make a drink.

HANNAH: In Chicago, our only friends were bartenders, and we only saw them when they were working.

PATRICK: God, do you ever get sick of repeating yourself?

HANNAH: It's true. We didn't have friends. We just had bartenders who had to talk to us because we were sitting at their bar.

PATRICK: We have no friends here.

HANNAH: Let's have a dinner party.

PATRICK: All people do is talk about their kids. Let's invite Trish and George for a visit.

HANNAH: The last time they visited us you ended up in the ER.

PATRICK: It was a poorly timed ulcer. It had nothing to do with their visit.

HANNAH: The three of you stayed up until four in the morning. You drank a bottle of scotch, two bottles of whiskey, and half a bottle of tequila. You literally vomited blood.

PATRICK: That's an exaggeration.

HANNAH: Trish is having another affair. Some nightclub owner or something. That's what she says anyway. I never know when she's telling the truth or when she's trying to shock me or impress me. I can't handle her when she's like this. All they do is fight, and then we fight, and then she says something nasty and you don't believe me. They're not good for us.

PATRICK: They're our oldest friends. They're part of my history. I can't conceive of a life in which they don't exist.

HANNAH: That sounds unhealthy.

PATRICK: I'm so unhappy.

HANNAH: Please, please consider seeing someone. You need someone to talk to.

PATRICK: I have a wife to talk to! What's the point of being married if I can't talk to you about this?

HANNAH: I feel like you want me to be as unhappy as you, and that's not fair.

PATRICK: You hate me.

HANNAH: I love you.

PATRICK: It doesn't feel like that right now.

HANNAH: You told me you'd see a therapist. You told me that. You promised.

PATRICK: And I will.

HANNAH: When?

PATRICK: Don't treat me like a child.

HANNAH: You'll see someone?

PATRICK: Yes. I mean, there are only hicks in this town, so I don't know how I'll find someone decent enough. But, sure, I'll find a hick therapist and I'll talk to them instead of to my wife.

HANNAH: So I'm not a nag, tell me when I can bring this up again.

PATRICK: Because you have no faith in me? Have some faith in me for once. Maybe that's part of the problem.

HANNAH: It's November. It's nearly Thanksgiving. Just give me a date.

PATRICK: How about February fourteenth?

HANNAH: Valentine's Day?

PATRICK: I hate this town.

SUMMER 1987—
TWENTY-EIGHT YEARS EARLIER, GRETA CATCHES
HANNAH UNDER HER MATTRESS

The sisters are alone in their father's house. Their father is . . . at work? At the tennis club? On a date? Greta has just knocked on Hannah's bedroom door and opened it. Hannah is under the bed, the mattress directly on top of her. Her head is turned to the side, facing the door.

GRETA: What are you doing?

HANNAH: Trying to kill myself.

GRETA: How did you do that?

HANNAH: I took out the slats.

GRETA: While you were already under the bed?

HANNAH: And then I lowered down the mattress.

GRETA: Does it hurt?

HANNAH: It's heavy.

GRETA: You're doing it wrong anyway.

HANNAH: How do you know?

GRETA: If you can breathe, it won't work. You have to turn your face up, toward the mattress. If you've got your head like that, you'll still be able to get air.

HANNAH: Oh.

GRETA: Door open or closed?

HANNAH: Closed.

DECEMBER 2013—
THE TWENTY-SEVENTH, HANNAH & PATRICK'S
FIRST WEDDING ANNIVERSARY

It's the third-coldest winter on record in Chicago. Temperatures have been averaging nineteen degrees. Outside, snow is falling. It's close to midnight. By morning, there will be eight fresh inches. Hannah and Patrick are in bed, covered head to foot in extra layers of clothing. Elmer is curled up beside them. He is kneading the comforter gently as he chases foxes in his dreams.

HANNAH: Do you love me?

PATRICK: Goofball, of course I do.

HANNAH: Since when?

PATRICK: Since forever.

HANNAH: Not true. There were others before me.

PATRICK: For a very long time, then.

HANNAH: Since when?

PATRICK: Remember your birthday?

HANNAH: Before we started dating?

PATRICK: My hair had finally grown back after the surgery. We were both single at the same time.

HANNAH: My mom and sister came to town to take me to dinner. It was the first birthday without Pops. It was a miserable birthday.

PATRICK: But I had a gig, and I couldn't come.

HANNAH: I don't think you were invited.

PATRICK: I wanted to do something special. I couldn't stand that you weren't coming to my show or that I wasn't having dinner with you. We'd been spending so much time together.

HANNAH: So many games of Scrabble.

PATRICK: I wanted to do something special, but you didn't

know what restaurant your family was taking you to, and so I called and called and called, and when that didn't work, just before my gig was supposed to start, I went to every restaurant on the Downtown Mall looking for you and your mother and your sister.

HANNAH: How many restaurants?

PATRICK: At least five or six before I found you.

HANNAH: But then you found me.

PATRICK: There you were. And I gave you the bottle of wine I'd bought earlier. But I couldn't stay. I was already late. So I gave you the bottle, and you didn't even stand up to hug me or thank me, but I think I knew you wanted to.

HANNAH: And then you left.

PATRICK: And then I left.

HANNAH: And my mother took the bottle of wine and looked at the label—

PATRICK: Faithful Hound.

HANNAH: —and said, 'That young man is in love with you.'

PATRICK: That's what Trish said, too.

HANNAH: Trish said, 'That young man is in love with you'?

PATRICK: She said, 'You're in love with her. You know that, right?'

HANNAH: And what did you say?

PATRICK: I'm sure I was very witty.

SPRING BREAK 2014—
HANNAH & TRISH AT A BAR IN CHARLOTTESVILLE

Twilight, what might rightly, but overly poetically, be called the gloaming. Patrick and George are at Fellini's, listening to a country band that Trish says she doesn't like.

TRISH: See that? That woman's forehead? See how smooth it is?

HANNAH: Yeah?

TRISH: That's Botox.

HANNAH: I never want to do Botox.

TRISH: You can get preemptive Botox. My brother told me. You can get Botox to make sure you don't get wrinkles. They do that now. You're telling me you wouldn't do that if you could?

HANNAH: It's botulism. You know that, right? You're basically injecting botulism into your forehead.

TRISH: I want it so bad. God, I wish I could afford it.

HANNAH: You can't?

TRISH: We're always broke.

HANNAH: But not *broke* broke.

TRISH: Month to month.

HANNAH: Us too.

TRISH: I hate being broke. I'd kill to own a home.

HANNAH: I'd kill to be out of debt. Where does it go?

TRISH: Booze, food, rent. I don't know. Guess how many times I've left my purse at a bar in the last month. I buy new purses like most people buy tubes of toothpaste.

HANNAH: That's funny.

TRISH: It isn't. Because if I'm lucky enough to find my purse the next day, then my wallet's gone. I haven't had an ID in years.

HANNAH: You flew to see us last year.

TRISH: I haven't had a wallet in a year, then.

HANNAH: Hmm. What if you get carded?

TRISH: I go to a different bar.

HANNAH: Hmm.

TRISH: But now I never pay more than twenty dollars for a purse. It's throwing away money. I love your purses. They look expensive.

HANNAH: I have only one purse.

TRISH: It looks expensive.

HANNAH: I got it on sale.

TRISH: I hate when you do that.

HANNAH: It's true.

TRISH: Not everything you buy can be on sale. You say that every time.

HANNAH: Do you ever feel like you tricked George into liking you?

TRISH: I can't even imagine what that would look like. How does one trick a man?

HANNAH: I used to like doing Patrick's laundry. Or, no. I did Patrick's laundry because I hoped he would like it, and then, obviously, he got used to it, and now I just really want him to do his own laundry. Should I have told him at the beginning that I didn't want to do his laundry? If I tricked him, it wasn't willful.

TRISH: What are we talking about here?

HANNAH: We're talking about laundry.

TRISH: Do you still like having sex with him?

HANNAH: I love having sex with him. Do you like having sex with George?

TRISH: I don't like having sex with anyone.

HANNAH: You told me that once before. I didn't take you seriously.

TRISH: It's so performative. All that moaning?

HANNAH: A person doesn't have to moan.

TRISH: All that talking? 'Take my cock. Take my fat hard cock. Push your pussy onto my big hard cock.'

HANNAH: The bartender is looking at us.

TRISH: Because he wants to tell me I can ride his big thick cock.

HANNAH: Don't be funny when I'm drinking. My cheek muscles are stretched to capacity. I'm going to spit my beer all over this bar.

TRISH: All over my giant hard dick.

HANNAH: Patrick says he wants a baby.

TRISH: How unpleasant!

HANNAH: I knew I could get you to stop. What about George?

TRISH: He says he wants to put babies on me.

HANNAH: It's like they're trying to make us hate them.

TRISH: Let's make a pact.

HANNAH: Pinky swear.

TRISH: No babies.

JUNE 2016—
PATRICK ARRIVES AT GEORGE & TRISH'S
APARTMENT ALONE FOR THE FIRST TIME

Brooklyn, late afternoon. Trish lets Patrick in. His complexion is pale, almost yellow. His clothes smell like international travel. Trish is wearing a denim jumpsuit. There is no air mattress in sight.

TRISH: You can put your bags in the bedroom. How was Paris? Was it amazing? God! Did you take photos? I want to know everything. What are the women wearing? Flats? Yellow? How do they do their hair? I need to know! I can't believe you leave for Yaddo in one week. What a summer! Such an adventure!

PATRICK: Where's George?

TRISH: Long story. He'll meet us later. Are you jet-lagged? Do you need a nap? Did you drink on the plane?

PATRICK: Only a little. Let's go to a bar.

TRISH: You seem tipsy.

PATRICK: Not tipsy enough.

TRISH: Do you need a minute? To get ready? Do you want to shower? Have you talked to Hannah? Does she know you landed?

PATRICK: Hannah doesn't care where I am.

TRISH: Uh-oh.

PATRICK: Take me to a bar.

TRISH: What's up with you and Hannah?

PATRICK: What's up with you and George?

TRISH: Hmm.

PATRICK: What's that supposed to mean?

TRISH: I've never seen you like this before.

PATRICK: Like what?

TRISH: Hmm.

PATRICK: How am I?

TRISH: Flustered.

PATRICK: I'm not flustered.

TRISH: Your guard is down.

PATRICK: In what way?

TRISH: You never talk about Hannah like that.

PATRICK: I haven't talked about Hannah at all.

TRISH: You two are normally so closed off.

PATRICK: I'm not closed off.

TRISH: Wow.

PATRICK: Why are you smiling like that? What's that look?

TRISH: Follow me.

PATRICK: To a bar? I don't need a shower. I need a drink.

TRISH: Come in here.

PATRICK: In the bathroom?

TRISH: Just come here. Come right here and stand in front of me and look at yourself. Look at what I can see.

PATRICK: This is weird.

TRISH: You'll see it, too. I know. Trust me.

PATRICK: Has George moved out?

TRISH: Don't change the subject. Look at yourself. Look at your face. Are you looking?

PATRICK: You're touching me.

TRISH: Of course I'm touching you. I've touched you a thousand times.

PATRICK: Not like that.

TRISH: Shh. What do you see? Tell me.

PATRICK: Your hand in my hair.

TRISH: Shh. Not that. What do you see in your face?

PATRICK: That feels good.

TRISH: Of course it does. Do you know what I see?

PATRICK: You should keep doing that. Just like that. That feels so good. You feel so good.

TRISH: I see a man who's lost.

PATRICK: Yes.

TRISH: I see a man who's forgotten who he is.

PATRICK: Yes.

TRISH: I see a man who wants to be wanted.

PATRICK: Yes. Please. Yes.

TRISH: I want you.

PATRICK: Do you?

TRISH: Turn around.

SEPTEMBER 2015—
A YEAR EARLIER, HANNAH TRIES TO GET
PATRICK'S ATTENTION

Patrick's home office. House in Kentucky. Second floor. Hannah in the doorway. Patrick sitting sideways at the computer, dobro on his thigh.

HANNAH: Knock, knock.

PATRICK: Oh. Wow. Um. You're naked.

HANNAH: Almost naked.

PATRICK: Those are some very pink panties.

HANNAH: They're new.

PATRICK: I assume so.

HANNAH: Want to take them off?

PATRICK: It's just . . .

HANNAH: Is this a bad time? I thought because . . . I heard you playing dobro, so I knew you weren't writing or grading, so I just thought . . .

PATRICK: I really want to learn this piece, you know?

HANNAH: Oh.

PATRICK: Don't feel bad. Okay?

HANNAH: Sure. Of course. No.

PATRICK: You understand, right? I'm just distracted right now.

HANNAH: Sure.

PATRICK: Don't cry. Are you crying?

HANNAH: I'm not crying.

PATRICK: Because it looks like—

HANNAH: I'm embarrassed. Argh. Kill me. This is mortifying.

PATRICK: Babe, don't be em—

HANNAH: Never mind. Forget it. Forget I tried. Please, promise me. Just forget I did this.

MARCH 2016—
SIX MONTHS LATER, PATRICK TRIES TO HAVE SEX WITH HANNAH AT A HOTEL IN LA

The bed Patrick and Hannah share is king-size; the room is airy and bright. The sheets are bleach-white and soft.

PATRICK: Good morning.

HANNAH: Hey.

PATRICK: How long have you been awake?

HANNAH: A few hours.

PATRICK: What have you been doing?

HANNAH: I went for a run. Then I stretched and showered and went for coffee.

PATRICK: You did not.

HANNAH: I did. I went for a run. Why would I make that up?

PATRICK: What did you do after?

HANNAH: I went to a panel, and after that I had a late breakfast down the street. I thought you'd be up, and you weren't. So I went to another panel, read the paper, and then I texted with Trish—she told me she's started shaving her face. Which I think is weird? But maybe it's not? Maybe it's good for exfoliation? My grandmother shaved her face. But I'm also surprised she told me. I would never admit that sort of thing to her. I'd be afraid she'd say something about it the next time we were together, and she'd be drunk. She'd wait until we had an audience, and then she'd announce it as a way to mock me. Did you know she's been shaving her arms for years? I didn't realize she was that hairy. I'm afraid I'll just stare the next time I see her. But maybe I should start shaving my face? I don't know. She said she misses us.

PATRICK: Please don't start shaving your face.

HANNAH: She's worried about George.

PATRICK: What about him?

HANNAH: I think their marriage is in real trouble. She wants to come down while we're in Charlottesville next week. But I told her not to.

PATRICK: Why'd you tell her that?

HANNAH: We'll be so busy. It's my sister's wedding. Between you and your cousin and me, it's going to be nonstop family.

PATRICK: How many miles did you run?

HANNAH: What are you doing?

PATRICK: I'm feeling your muscles. How many miles?

HANNAH: Can you stop that? Seven or eight. My watch died. Please stop.

PATRICK: Come here.

HANNAH: I'm right here. What are you doing?

PATRICK: Face me.

HANNAH: I'm reading something.

PATRICK: What are you reading?

HANNAH: The news.

PATRICK: You already read the news. Come here. Put your phone away. Lie down with me.

HANNAH: I'm sitting next to you. Isn't that enough?

PATRICK: I want you to lie next to me. Under the covers.

HANNAH: Please stop trying to take off my shirt.

PATRICK: Where are you right now?

HANNAH: I'm right here. I've been right here and awake for hours. Literally hours. It's midday. Stop it. What are you doing?

PATRICK: I'm trying to make love to my wife.

HANNAH: I can't.

PATRICK: You won't.

HANNAH: I'm not in the mood.

PATRICK: You're never in the mood.

HANNAH: You smell like booze. You smell like a bar. I'm serious. It's not your breath. It's your skin. It's your hair. The sheets smell like alcohol. Like old alcohol. It's not a turn-on.

PATRICK: Just stop.

HANNAH: I don't find this attractive. I'm not trying to be unkind. I'm not trying to humiliate you, but I don't want to be some woman who pretends to be interested in sex and then spends the rest of the day filled with resentment and self-loathing because she didn't want to do it.

PATRICK: You make it sound like I'm raping you.

HANNAH: No.

PATRICK: I'm your husband.

HANNAH: I'm not interested.

PATRICK: You were always interested before.

HANNAH: Maybe I was. I don't know.

PATRICK: What are you saying?

HANNAH: Maybe I was interested and maybe I wasn't. I don't know. Maybe there were times when I pretended to be interested and I shouldn't have. Maybe it's my fault.

AUGUST 2016—
HANNAH & HER SISTER & THEIR MOTHER TALK
ABOUT BLOWJOBS

Someone's kitchen table. A bottle of wine. Three glasses. Maybe two bottles of wine.

HANNAH: What do you mean you've never given a blowjob you didn't want to give?

GRETA: I can barely keep from choking when I *want* to do it.

HANNAH: Are you trying to make me feel self-conscious?

GRETA: You're saying you were forced?

HANNAH: No. Not physically forced. But I've definitely gone down on a man when I didn't want to.

GRETA: Why?

HANNAH: —

GRETA: How?

HANNAH: —

MOTHER: I know what your sister means.

GRETA: You do?

MOTHER: Of course. I'm a woman.

GRETA: Are you two nuts?

MOTHER: Men have ways.

GRETA: What ways?

MOTHER: Moping, begging.

HANNAH: Yes. Right. That's what I mean.

GRETA: I am aghast. Absolutely aghast.

SEPTEMBER 2016—
HANNAH IS ON THE PHONE WITH HER BROTHER

Hannah is alone in her kitchen in Kentucky, her phone cradled between her ear and her shoulder. She has been divorced for one month. Now she's standing in front of the refrigerator; its doors are open. There are eggs and there is cheese and there are many bottles of hot sauce. She dreads nighttime meals most of all, this new calculation of putting together a reasonable portion for one.

BROTHER: Remember how you said once you didn't get enough love?

HANNAH: What are you talking about? What are you having for dinner?

BROTHER: About when we were little, you said once that you didn't get as much love as Greta and I got. From our parents.

HANNAH: I said that? Do you think it's okay to eat eggs for more than one meal in the same day?

BROTHER: Probably not. You said you thought you didn't get as much love from Mom and Dad.

HANNAH: Maybe I'll have cheese and crackers?

BROTHER: That's not a meal. You're not getting enough protein from cheese and crackers. But I think you're right.

HANNAH: About what?

BROTHER: I don't think you got as much love.

HANNAH: We should run another marathon.

SUMMER 2017—
HANNAH & HER MOTHER ARE DRINKING
CHAMPAGNE; TRISH & PATRICK WALK BY

It's ninety-seven degrees out. Elmer is still alive. Hannah's mother moved to Lexington only a few months ago. They've taken to weekly happy hour outings at a little French place downtown. Between sips, Hannah catches a glimpse of a woman who could only be Trish standing outside the bar. Over the next year and a half, Hannah will see Patrick many more times—on campus, during department meetings, for coffee—until sometime during fall semester 2019, when he'll quit his job in Kentucky and move back to Charlottesville for good. She won't ever be able to say for sure when the last time she saw him was—what he was wearing, whether or not they said hello, whether or not they even smiled at each other. But without a doubt, this is about to be Hannah's last encounter ever with Trish. Of course, she doesn't know this yet.

HANNAH: Don't turn around.

MOTHER: What?

HANNAH: Christ. I told you not to turn around.

MOTHER: That's like telling someone not to think about elephants. Oh! Is that Trish? Oh! Is that Patrick?

HANNAH: Did they see you?

MOTHER: I'm afraid it's worse than that.

HANNAH: Tell me they aren't coming in here.

MOTHER: They aren't coming in.

HANNAH: Thank god.

MOTHER: They're already inside.

HANNAH: Jesus, *Mom*!

MOTHER: They're standing right behind you.

PATRICK: Ladies!

HANNAH: Wow. Hey. Wild. Weird.

MOTHER: Patrick. And, Trish?

TRISH: Hi. Yes, it's Trish. We've met.

MOTHER: Yes. You were at the wedding if I remember correctly.

TRISH: —

HANNAH: —

PATRICK: What are you two doing here?

MOTHER: Happy hour.

PATRICK: I heard you moved to town. What do you think?

MOTHER: Right now I think it's small.

PATRICK: We're doing a bit of moving and unpacking ourselves.

HANNAH: Both of you?

PATRICK: We found a place just around the corner from here. We're giving Lexington a try.

TRISH: We've been unpacking boxes all day.

HANNAH: —

MOTHER: —

TRISH: Our apartment is full of books. It's kind of crazy how many we have.

MOTHER: Bugs? Your apartment is full of bugs?

TRISH: *Books.* It's full of *books.*

MOTHER: What a remarkable thing to say.

HANNAH: Remarkable.

MOTHER: I could have sworn I heard 'bugs.'

TRISH: Patrick?

PATRICK: We heard the new cantina down the block is good. We're headed there now. Zero food in our fridge with the move.

TRISH: Patrick?

HANNAH: They're closed.

PATRICK: Already?

HANNAH: Only on Tuesdays.

TRISH: Patrick?

PATRICK: Maybe we'll snag a seat at the bar here, then. You two wouldn't mind, would you?

HANNAH: —

MOTHER: —

TRISH: Patrick, it's time to leave.

PATRICK: I guess we'll be seeing you, then.

HANNAH: Be seeing you.

TRISH: See ya later.

MOTHER: *See ya later.*

HANNAH: Hm.

MOTHER: *Hm.*

HANNAH: Did you really think she said their apartment was filled with 'bugs'?

MOTHER: I'm hard of hearing.

HANNAH: You didn't hear her say 'books'? You never admit to being hard of hearing.

MOTHER: I'm just a dotty old woman.

HANNAH: You never admit to being old. I can't believe they live here now.

MOTHER: Together even.

HANNAH: The last time I saw her was right here. At this bar. Isn't that funny?

MOTHER: We might have conflicting appreciations of *funny.*

HANNAH: I wouldn't mind if that's the last time I see her.

MOTHER: Or Patrick.

HANNAH: Yeah. Or Patrick. Him too.

APRIL 2008—
YEARS AND YEARS AND YEARS EARLIER, PATRICK & HANNAH DECIDE TO LIVE TOGETHER, AND AN IMAGINED PATRICK INTERRUPTS THE NARRATIVE

Patrick is making cocktails. Hannah is deveining shrimp. They're in his kitchen in Charlottesville—what will soon be her kitchen, too. But when the camera zooms out, we see that the kitchen is really just a set piece, and the set piece is in Hannah's hollowed-out brain, and Hannah is at her desk in Kentucky. And she is alone.

PATRICK: We should celebrate.

HANNAH: I mean, I've practically been living here already, right? So nothing will change. Everything will be the same. Isn't that what we want? For nothing to change?

PATRICK: We should get some champagne. Maybe two bottles of champagne. We could throw a party.

HANNAH: How often will your parents visit? Are you sure they don't want me to pay them rent? Will they be like room-mates?

PATRICK: They'll probably visit all the time now.

HANNAH: So they *will* be like roommates. Is that strange?

PATRICK: They love you. They're going to want to be here all the time.

HANNAH: —

PATRICK: Are you having second thoughts? Come here. Sit on my lap. Man, your ass is bony. Maybe sit right here, beside me, on the bench. Don't pretend to be mad. I can see you're trying not to smile. It'll be fun. It'll be a riot. They're not like normal parents. You know that.

HANNAH: I like your dad a lot.

PATRICK: Does that mean you don't like my mother?

HANNAH: I love your mom. She's intense.

PATRICK: What's that a euphemism for?

HANNAH: Are you baiting me? Are you trying to start a fight?

PATRICK: We don't fight.

HANNAH: Of course we fight.

PATRICK: We don't. You don't let us. You acquiesce to everything.

HANNAH: We fight about Trish and George.

PATRICK: I don't want to talk about them.

HANNAH: See?

PATRICK: You're changing the subject.

HANNAH: I'm not sure I am.

PATRICK: Why don't you like my mom?

HANNAH: I adore your mom. I wish she wouldn't try to sell me on having kids every time I see her.

PATRICK: She doesn't do that every time.

HANNAH: Literally every time I see her she tells me that a woman feels differently when the baby is hers. What she doesn't understand is that I like other people's babies. Other people's babies are enchanting. You can hand them off whenever you want. It's my own baby I'd hate. And we do, too, fight. We fight about Holly.

PATRICK: But not in a real way.

HANNAH: I think it's weird that she walks into your house whenever she wants, as though she still lives here. I'm not worried you have lingering feelings or anything.

PATRICK: But I do have feelings for her. I care for her.

HANNAH: But not romantically.

PATRICK: No. Not romantically. But I worry about her. Did I tell you that she wanted me to promise not to marry the very next person I lived with after her?

HANNAH: Did you promise?

PATRICK: I did.

HANNAH: —

PATRICK: Are you upset?

HANNAH: I'm the very next person you're living with after Holly. Does that mean we can't get married? I feel like maybe you're trying to upset me?

PATRICK: All I'm saying is that I care for her; I worry about her. She's ten years older than we are. She never had kids. She never got married. She thought she was going to have those things with me.

HANNAH: Sometimes I think you enjoy worrying about people, that you find comfort in taking care of people, that you might prefer the wounded or hopeless type.

PATRICK: You're not the wounded or hopeless type.

HANNAH: But I'm shy. I'm reserved. I'm quiet. All of which might translate as overlapping symptoms of the wounded and hopeless type.

PATRICK: Holly isn't shy or quiet.

HANNAH: No. She's loud and obnoxious and a total addict.

PATRICK: She's not an addict. I know addicts. She's not an addict.

HANNAH: We can agree to disagree.

PATRICK: —

HANNAH: I'm uneasy just asking you this . . .

PATRICK: Don't be timid. I hate it when you're timid.

HANNAH: I really wish you'd ask her not to come over unannounced anymore. Especially since I'm moving in. It's not normal that she keeps a closet full of clothes at her ex-boyfriend's house. She's going to continue coming over as long as they're here. She'll always have an excuse to stop by whenever she wants. You see that, right?

PATRICK: I don't want to hurt her feelings.

HANNAH: What about my feelings? Why would you privilege an ex-girlfriend's feelings over a current girlfriend's request?

PATRICK: No.

HANNAH: What?

PATRICK: No. Nope. Not in a million years.

HANNAH: Not in a million years? I'm lost.

PATRICK: Absolutely not. Totally false. I disagree.

HANNAH: You disagree with what?

PATRICK: You would never actually have asked me such a direct question. *Back then* . . . You wouldn't have been so vulnerable and open, so I'm not going to answer it. You might have wondered silently to yourself, but you never would have made that request aloud—not to 'privilege an ex-girlfriend's feelings' over your own . . . You'd have been too panicked about my reaction.

HANNAH: I . . .

PATRICK: *This* is why we never fought, not at first. You bottled up everything, saving every offense of mine for some moment in the future when you'd finally have stopped loving me, and then—with stunning and nearly pathological recollection— you would bring every transgression back to the surface, offering it all up triumphantly like some freshly discovered box of decade-old evidence. That's what you're doing now.

HANNAH: But this is *my* version of events. You're not allowed to interrupt.

PATRICK: Then get it right. Tell the truth at least. If you're going to talk for me—and without my permission—then you should also try to represent yourself as accurately as possible if the objective is to figure us out, to figure out where we went wrong and how you did or didn't get us there.

HANNAH: You're right. I'm sorry. I agree with you.

PATRICK: You wouldn't have said that either. You never admitted you were wrong back then. You could and would deliver up a weepy-eyed apology. But you never actually admitted to being wrong.

HANNAH: I know. You're right about that, too. And I'm sorry. I really am. But this is who I am now. This is me *now*, speaking to the you that might have been.

PATRICK: I wonder how long we might have lasted if you'd been able to be wrong.

HANNAH: Each breakup makes a person better. Something Trish once said to me, and I hate that it was Trish who said it, because I recall this conversation with greater frequency than I'd care to admit, because it's clearly resonated as one of those obvious life truths that a person can go a lifetime without ever articulating—

PATRICK: You're losing me.

HANNAH: Remember that kid Trish lived with before she and George got together? He followed her to Charlottesville just to be with her. He was independently wealthy. Or, rather, his father was wealthy. We called him the trust funder. He didn't have a job.

PATRICK: That kid was fresh out of college.

HANNAH: Right. He was at least five years younger than we were, and, behind her back, we talked about how bizarre it was that she was dating someone so young.

PATRICK: Sure. I remember this kid.

HANNAH: One night after they broke up, Trish got a little wistful and she told me how funny and depressing she thought breakups were.

PATRICK: Of course. Breakups are depressing. There isn't anything particularly profound or memorable about what you're telling me.

HANNAH: She went on to speculate about the kid's future wife, and how this future, currently nonexistent woman would always have Trish to thank.

PATRICK: Because Trish broke up with him, thereby making him available?

HANNAH: No! Because Trish helped turn him into a good man. All the little things he hadn't known to do before he lived with her—everything from putting the toilet seat down to folding her underwear to where to put his fingers when they had sex—she'd taught him all these things, and by the time they broke up, in many ways, he was kind of perfect for Trish.

PATRICK: Trish said this?

HANNAH: She did! She said this! But she was unable to take advantage of what a well-suited man he'd become because she could no longer find him attractive in the right way. She couldn't unremember all the ways she'd trained him. She couldn't shake the fact that she was responsible for his education in how to be a good man. So she broke up with him. Even though he hadn't done anything wrong, even though he'd actually done everything she asked of him.

PATRICK: You're trying to connect this to me, but I don't see it.

HANNAH: You're going to say I'm being callous.

PATRICK: Just say it.

HANNAH: You'll accuse me of being something I'm trying not to be.

PATRICK: Call it a catch-22, then, but don't be a coward now. Say it.

HANNAH: I don't think I made you a better man.

PART TWO

AN IMAGINED EXCHANGE

A few weeks ago, I heard from a friend that Holly had over-dosed. She was fifty-one years old. The news was a totally unex-pected blow, and I couldn't get you out of my thoughts. You didn't text. You didn't call. It was completely unlike you—or, to be more accurate, completely unlike *my* version of you—not to take advantage of a tragedy in order to be in touch, whereby you'd have had an opportunity to be melancholic, mawkish even. I was surprised. To be honest, I was upset. I started won-dering about your parents, to whom I'd once been so close, and whether or not you'd at least reach out when *they* died. After that, my thoughts spiraled, and I found myself contemplat-ing the future funerals of everyone we'd ever had in common. When would a death finally bring us back together? Not *together* together. But I wondered what event would ultimately bring our orbits into view again. Eventually, my admittedly indulgent fantasies landed on my own mother. During our marriage, she'd been smitten with you and you with her. She sobbed when I told her we were splitting up. You two had lunch to hash out the whys and hows of your affair. It took her three years to actu-ally remove you from her will. Will I call you when she dies? Will I text? Or will you hear the news from Hugh or from my brother-in-law? And when you hear the news, will you call me? Will I answer? Who can say? My point here is that Holly's death sent me down an unexpected wormhole of nostalgia, and for a little while—because you hadn't contacted me, because you hadn't used her death as an excuse to reconnect with your past (*this* past)—I believed that you'd changed in some fundamental way. This very likely possibility stunned me. But then, not three nights ago, you texted—after almost two years and out of the blue!—to ask if a phishing attempt regarding an obviously bogus Home Depot order was mine. I wasn't going to respond—there's no way you could have believed the order was real—but in the end, I couldn't resist: *Don't click the link! Scam. Not for me. Thx for asking.* Your response was immediate and Essential Patrick, a spectacularly distilled blend of irony and insecurity from a hipster who never wanted to be regarded as a hipster: *Thumbs-up emoji.* There you were, the old you, and I knew you hadn't changed. It was comforting in its way, knowing you were still you.

YOU: I disagree with much of how you've portrayed me.

Well, sure. Yeah. That makes sense.

YOU: Don't condescend to me.

Wherever I go, there I am.

YOU: Let's start with my affair.

That only seems right.

YOU: Your insistence that Trish made the first move is entirely wrong. I dislike that you've included a fictionalized version of the event that contradicts my own account. Your narrative—that I got off the plane from Paris and that she stood me in front of a mirror and started groping my hair—that's one hundred percent fantasy. We got drunk, I touched her foot with mine under the table, she responded. We were at a bar. George was with us. He missed everything. The secrecy was half the turn-on. After that, things happened quickly.

But that she was responsive at all . . . You were married to her best friend. She was married to yours. She had no right.

> YOU: You didn't want to have sex with me. You also didn't want anyone else to have sex with me.

I've considered that possibility. Maybe it's a female problem. I'm not saying men don't also get bored. Of course they do. But there's something that happens to women in long-term monogamous relationships. At least, I'm assuming I'm not the only one. Maybe I am, which is a lonely thought, but my assumption is that it's what a lot of us do: we fall in love with a man, and then—out of fear of losing him, out of determination to win, or maybe to prove some sort of female supremacy by nailing down the guy who everyone else couldn't—we make ourselves invaluable. We do the laundry; we do the cleaning. We say, when the man tries to help, 'I don't mind! I like it! It's easy for me!' And the man, happy not to help, because who wouldn't want to be waited on if they could and for free—

> YOU: I know hundreds of women who would pull their hair out—or, as you might say, chew their hands

off—if they were accused of behavior as backward as this. Those same women would also probably tell you to grow a pair and stop taking care of men. This is a problem you alone create. This isn't women.

Let me finish. So there's this man who has allowed himself to become a kind of fatted hen—

> YOU: That's not a thing. 'Fatted hen' is not a known idiom. You still speak like a foreign mistress from a Roth novel. It's endearing.

So there's this man who's allowed himself to get comfortable, and, of course, there's also this woman who has encouraged the man to get comfortable. Days go by. Weeks go by. Eventually months and years go by. One day, the woman looks up from the sink and sees her reflection in the dark of the glass—

> YOU: This is very Atwood, very 'The Female Body.'

—and she hears her husband upstairs in the second bedroom, which was turned into his study even though she's the published author and not him, and he's playing his stupid fucking dobro again with its tinny fucking sound that makes her want to grind her knuckles into shards of glass, and she thinks to herself, *Why the fuck am I doing these dishes?* But it doesn't end there; the madness doesn't stop, because the woman, after this first night, doesn't say anything. She doesn't let her grievances be known. Instead, she thinks, *Well, after all, when I clean the dishes, they actually get clean, and when I fold the clothes, they actually get folded, and anyway, if I don't start the next load, it'll be days before he does, and I want to wear that shirt tomorrow, so I guess I'll go ahead and do it myself, and really, what's the big deal?* She talks herself down that first night, scrubbing and wiping and spraying and putting away, and by bedtime the hysteria has dissipated. The problem is, it happens again a few nights later, and then again the night after that. Suddenly, though she's started muttering vague dissatisfactions under her breath when he goes right up the stairs after dinner and she knows he can hear the muttering, it's happening all the time. All she can think now is *Why the fuck?* There isn't even a fundament.

YOU: You learned that word from me.

To be honest, he doesn't even have to do anything wrong anymore. He can, for instance, make her a smoothie and hand it to her just after she's home from a long run, and, as she accepts it, she looks over his shoulder at the Vitamix with a viscous green goo dripping down its sides, the vegetable debris scattered all across the counter, the coconut water with its lid off . . . All she can think is *Why the fuck?* And so maybe this is where he begins to detect there might actually be something wrong, something missing, something he can't quite put his finger on. At first, he doesn't try to talk about it either. Talking is just so direct, you know? Instead, he starts doing 'nice' things for her. He buys her flowers. He brings her a glass of wine while she's reading at her tiny desk, which is shoved between the television and the bookcase in the corner of the living room. He rubs her feet while they watch a show. He kisses her shoulder for no reason at all. But no matter how many of these nice gestures he performs, the thing that's missing remains missing. It's like there's a deadness all over her skin, in her eyes, in her voice even. And so, finally, feeling like he's going a little mad himself, having become so accustomed to the way she'd previously adored him, having in fact learned to take that adoration for granted, he asks her, 'Are you okay?' And she says, 'Of course.' And he says, 'It's just—' And she says, 'Really. I'm fine. I promise. I'm fine.' But all the while, all that's there, all that's going on in her mind at all is *Why the fuck? Why the fuck? Why the fuck?* A freight train of hatred roaring in her brain. Then one night, because she's told him she's okay and because, truth be told, he's gotten kind of used to the vacancy in her eyes and voice— maybe he even likes it? Because this version does seem a little less opinionated than her prototype?—he slips his hand under her tank top after she's turned off the bedside lamp and then tries to run his fingers down the length of her torso and under the elastic of her underwear. But this is the last straw. This is the thing she doesn't want to fake anymore, and so she doesn't. Simple as that. Her hand grabs for his before his fingers can push her apart, and she finally screams aloud the words that have been with her for so long now. *'WHY THE FUCK?'*

> YOU: Wow. You actually hated me. I hadn't realized that before. Wow.

I hated *me.*

> YOU: You know what I dislike about this exercise?

I suspect you'll tell me.

> YOU: Even now, you deny me any agency. Whether it's intentional or not, whether you can even see it hap-

pening or not, you have always found ways to emasculate and degrade me. You folded my clothes? You did my dishes? Big deal. It's not like I didn't know how. I did! I took care of myself before I met you.

Arguable.

YOU: I paid my bills. I cleaned my own home. You took those things over, and I let you. But you didn't do it out of some misplaced urgency to keep me around or so I'd need you—you did it because you thought you could do it better. You didn't trust me to pay the bills. You didn't trust me to fold the clothes to your precise and uptight standards. The truth is, I wanted to fuck Trish. I'd wanted to fuck her for years. I liked flirting with her, and I liked knowing how much she wanted me. It actually made being friends with George easier. I liked him more, knowing that his wife and I wanted each other. It also made being married to you easier. Do you know how stuck-up you are? Do you know how persnickety and OCD your habits and predilections have become? And you encouraged me to buy the dobro. You encouraged me to learn a new instrument. You're complicit in this. You make it sound like I was some solipsistic asshole lording my indifference over you, but you went out of your way to make yourself uncomfortable as though it proved you were stronger than other people, stronger than me. Well, guess what? Putting up with someone else's bullshit when you're not happy doesn't mean you're strong, it means you're a coward for not stopping it.

Fine. Let's talk about the dobro.

> YOU: The dobro isn't the point.

The dobro is everything. It's our marriage in a nutshell. I encouraged you to buy it, yes. I encouraged you to learn it, because you weren't writing or, when you were, it was the same book you'd been working on for years. You were circling the drain.

> YOU: That book was like a child to me. It had an agent.
> It had people who believed in it. A few editors were
> on the fence. It had life left in it.

Do you remember *when* you decided to start writing stories? It was when I got published in *McSweeney's*.

> YOU: Wrong. I was a writer before I ever met you.

It's like you took one look at me—simple, boring, uptight me—and thought, *Jesus, if she can do it, then surely so can I.* I got my first story published, and that's when you decided to start writing and submitting stories of your own. But nothing got taken; nothing got published. Do you remember? Do you remember how you finally started getting published?

> YOU: This is gross. I feel dirty even tolerating this con-
> versation.

You asked me to ask one of the editors who'd just bought a story from me. Your request was so deflating, but I couldn't say no. You made me feel it was my job as your girlfriend to prop you up. You practically dictated the email. Again and again, after every one of my publications, it was assumed I would email the editor and ask about you. When I didn't, you sulked. When I did, I felt beat down. You emasculated yourself. It wasn't me. You wanted to cut to the front of the line; you wanted the reward without the work. The day I sold my first novel, do you remember what you said?

> YOU: You are a Rolodex of discontentment and perceived slights.

You said, 'What does this mean for me?' At dinner, to celebrate, you drank too much, and you brooded even more. You kept talking about all the ways this boon for me was going to leave you in the dust.

> YOU: And I was right.

The next day you started writing a novel. All over again, I could practically hear you thinking it—*If she can do it, then so can I . . .*

> YOU: I didn't start writing it the next day. Not everything needs to be so theatrical and reactive. I'd been thinking about a novel of my own for a long time. Instead of assuming I was responding to your success with envy and jealousy, why not assume that I was inspired? That your good fortune was motivation to stop my daydreaming and start writing in earnest?

Because that's when you started treating me badly. That's when the first change occurred.

YOU: If I was such a monster, then why didn't you leave?

The joke of it is that this all happened *before* we got married. This happened *before* you went to grad school in Boston, *before* I moved to Chicago. I used to think the most irrational thing I'd ever done was stay with Stephen Strange six years *after* he told me he couldn't say for sure whether I was smart or not because he couldn't gauge the intelligence of women in general.

> YOU: I never doubted your intelligence. And I always admired your writing. It's something I loved about you immediately. You're right: I was envious of it and of your success, but I was also proud of you. I thought you knew that. It came so easily to you. You'd just sit down and write. For me, it was a chore. And it felt like, whenever I looked up, there you were with a new book deal.

I was bulimic on and off the entire time we were together.

> YOU: I didn't . . . You never . . . I don't know what to say.

I had very real struggles of my own. I just didn't share them.

> YOU: Fuck, I'd give us back our thirties if I could.

I don't *want* them back. Nothing would change, because you're right: I was and am hyper neurotic, and I did and do have grotesquely rigid expectations. My own way of being virtually precludes a successful relationship. I'm morbidly secretive, but

I expect unmitigated honesty and complete transparency from everyone else.

> YOU: It's nice to hear you admit to being secretive. I appreciate that. I didn't always know what the secrets were, but I knew you were keeping them. I really didn't know about the vomiting. I wouldn't have ignored that. I would have wanted to help you. I've always thought you had a beautiful body. I liked it when you put on weight.

I know that, and I'm grateful. But your reverence couldn't compete with my self-loathing. Every morning, before I'd even gotten out of bed, I'd grope and pinch and clamp my thighs, my sides, my hip bones, my rib cage. Sometimes I could go months without puking. But then something would happen— we'd go out and I'd have one bite too many, and instead of stopping, I'd have twenty more bites and feel bloated and distended and like I might pass out from the pain, and so I'd shove my fingers down my throat. It's a lot like being a drunk. You fall off the wagon and you think, *Well, the clock has to start over now anyway, so I might as well enjoy myself for a little while before it does* . . . But then, also like a drunk, you get clean and you begin to count the days, and you feel really good and proud of yourself. You think, *This is the year I won't do it once.* But then there's a provocation, and it happens again, and on and on and on.

> YOU: What do you think would have happened if you'd told me?

Honestly? I didn't trust you not to have the same reaction as Stephen Strange. I didn't trust you not to find my openness, but also my vulnerability, sexy. I didn't want to be fixed by you. I suppose I didn't want to be supported by you either.

> YOU: Trish needs me.

You told me that once.

> YOU: A lot of bad things happened to her when she and George were in New York.

She did a lot of those bad things to herself.

> YOU: She makes me feel wanted. Better than that, she makes me feel needed.

I didn't want that kind of relationship. I didn't want to be with someone who couldn't stand up on his own.

> YOU: And maybe that's exactly what I did want.

Do you remember our wedding?

> YOU: You and I decided not to drink a lot that day or in the days leading up to it. We took it seriously.

That's right.

> YOU: We didn't want a priest or some stranger to marry us, so you asked your brother. But he wasn't ordained,

so we had to do it officially in town the day before
with the sheriff. You started shaking and bawling, and
you turned bright red. It was such an intense display
of emotion. It scared me.

And you were goofy, jokey, and the sheriff was clearly unnerved
by us both. But we were unnerved by him. He had a gun in his
holster!

> YOU: The next day, on what I considered our real wed-
> ding day because our friends and family were with us,
> we switched roles. I was a weepy mess, and you were
> stoic and unmoved.

I was moved.

> YOU: It was a great day. One of the greatest of my life.

And then what happened?

> YOU: We stayed in Charlottesville for the weekend at a
> hotel in town. Trish and George booked a room. Your
> sister booked a room. We all had dinner together, but
> afterward you went back to the hotel with Greta, and
> I stayed out with Trish and George.

You stayed out and . . .

> YOU: Trish got so drunk that she climbed up a brick
> wall and tried to do a flip. When the back of her head
> hit the pavement, I thought she was dead. I think

we all thought for a second she was dead. But she wasn't even bleeding. And when she jumped up, she laughed, and then we all laughed, and we went to another bar.

I remember having very complicated feelings about that scene when you told me the next morning. Something was wrong—with her, with you, with all of us.

YOU: She wasn't trying to hurt you when she said she'd met someone who made her want to have babies. She was nervous. We were both hopped up on sex and tension and energy. We also—I know this is a strange or even disturbing thing to suggest—I think we both missed you. For years, whenever we'd visit them in New York, it would always be all four of us together. Even though there were times when one of us might storm off after a fight or after getting too drunk—

I literally never once stormed off. That was never me. It was only ever Trish.

YOU: The point is, we'd always all four be together in the morning for brunch and champagne and another full day of drinking and looking at art and exploring the city. But that was the summer you chose not to come with me to my friend's wedding in Colombia. We had a chance to be together for a week, a kind of long-belated honeymoon after too many years, but you didn't even consider coming with me.

You promised me you'd see a therapist; you didn't. By Valentine's, you still hadn't. I felt raw and betrayed and tired. By March, when you started to plan the Colombia trip, the last thing in the world I wanted was to fly to another country with you.

> YOU: You encouraged me to go away for the summer. You practically begged me to leave you alone.

We were fighting constantly. You were moping. I thought we'd both be well served by a break. You got residencies in France and at Yaddo for nearly the entire summer. I assumed you wanted to get away from Kentucky. Those residencies were proof that you were working on something special.

> YOU: You could have let me come home after France, but you said the flights into Kentucky were too expensive. Such bullshit. You just wanted more time without me. You made me go to New York instead. You made me stay there without you for one week instead of being with you, which is where I should have been. You set me up. You set *us* up, Trish and me.

You sound dangerously close to accusing me of making you cheat.

> YOU: I'm trying to explain the circumstances. I'm trying to reveal to you how I felt, how *you* made me feel that summer. You made me feel unwanted. Trish made me feel desired. Your absence unsettled us all—George, Trish, me. Something was shifting. I suppose Trish

and I felt like we were sinking, and we grabbed on to each other before we went down.

Can we include the fact that George was practically living with another woman when you landed in New York and that, when you realized this, you chose not to stay with Hugh as had been the plan all along, but instead to stay with Trish? I'm just saying, for someone who asked for his agency to be acknowledged, you're now annoyingly willing to duck blame. I reject your theory that Trish was nervous when she called to tell me about the new man in her life. I reject that a bad case of the jitters accounts for the photos she sent me of the two of you doing laundry, reading in coffee shops, having glasses of wine.

> YOU: We missed you. She missed you. She talked about you all the time.

She was gloating. And you were either too drunk and oblivious to see it, or you've been duped by an even more outrageous storyteller than me.

> YOU: It hurt my feelings when you told me you didn't want to have children. And then, suddenly, there was Trish, whispering in my ear, telling me how great I was, saying you were crazy for not wanting my kids. That very first night, she was all in. It was intoxicating. It still is.

I tried to have an affair. In Chicago, I considered it. I wanted to do something so awful that I'd have to leave you. I wanted to betray you in an unforgivable way. I was too weak to break up with you, but I thought maybe I could muster the courage to have sex with someone else.

YOU: And did you?

No. We moved to Lexington, and things got better for a little while. We were both so shocked by what was missing in Kentucky that in those early days it was you and me clinging to each other like life preservers. We had sex all the time. We touched each other like people new to being in a couple. That, to me, was intoxicating.

YOU: But then we fucked up. We decided to spend our first summer back in Chicago.

We packed up the car, packed up Elmer, and we moved back temporarily. But the city had changed. We'd changed. The Airbnb was a dump, a favorite word of yours, one that started out funny but then, as time went on, became a weight on my shoulders.

YOU: It *was* a dump.

Everything became a dump in your eyes, Lexington especially. We powered through the summer, but that's when the closeness we'd shared started to fade. You wanted to write at coffee shops all day and then go out every night, which of course was putting a strain on us financially.

YOU: You were always thinking about money.

You promised we'd spend less when we went home in the fall. But there was also Elmer to consider. If we stayed out all day and then went out at night, he'd be alone. So I was the one to stay with him. I was the one to walk him, feed him. You put me in the position of having to be the responsible caretaker. My resentment accumulated, and I started to change. I started to want different things and to be willing to say that I wanted different things.

   YOU: So what?

I guess what I'm trying to figure out is, whose fault is it? Mine for changing or yours for not changing? You had to have everything your way, and I accommodated you until one day I couldn't. So, whose fault is it?

   YOU: You're looking at it wrong. Forget about who
       changed and who didn't. That doesn't matter. At the
       end of the day—another favorite saying of yours—it's
       your fault for marrying me. From everything you've
       said, it's evident that you were, at best, on the fence
       about me when I proposed. You're the one who said
       yes. I was all in then.

After we divorced, we promised that we'd be the ones to tell each other when something big happened in our lives. Because we were still family—my sister marrying your cousin, plus his parents are so close to yours—we never wanted to hear secondhand about something meaningful. It would have been too heartbreaking. But that's exactly what ended up happening. You and Trish got married in Chicago on New Year's Eve, and my sister was the one to tell me, having heard about it from her husband, who'd heard about it from his mother, who'd heard about it from yours. I guess all I'm trying to say is, you've hurt my feelings, too. Sure, I didn't want to have your kids even before you cheated. But that also wasn't a secret. I tried to get sterilized when I was thirty. You knew that. That was years before we got married. It seems unfair to count a preexisting resolution as a deliberate attack on either your feelings or your masculinity.

YOU: But you told Trish that another man might have made you feel differently.

I hate that you know that. You shouldn't know that. But it was also conjecture; it was purely hypothetical. She'd been complaining about George, so I reciprocated by complaining about you. That's when she said she'd met someone who made her want babies. She was talking about you, by the way, which obviously I didn't know. And so I told her that, in a different life, I could imagine having made different decisions. I never suggested you were the only reason I didn't have them. But, fine, yes, if what you're after here is my acknowledgment that your unpredictability and irresponsibility frightened me, then yes, absolutely, I admit it.

YOU: But now you own a home with a man who has a kid. You're helping raise a child now. Can you imagine how that makes me feel? Trish and I tried. You think we manufactured wanting to have children as an excuse for cheating, but you're wrong.

There's something I never told you.

YOU: There must be a million things by now.

Yes, but back then, about that day when I told Trish that a different man might have made me want different things.

YOU: Yes?

After she and I hung up, I called you. You were at Yaddo, and your line was busy. I tried you two or three more times quickly, never leaving a message because I knew you'd see my missed calls and call me back eventually.

YOU: And did I?

About ten minutes later, yes. You were angry and short with me. I didn't ask you to explain. I told you about my call with Trish—some of it anyway—including the fact that she'd told me George was seeing some new girl on the side. Without missing a beat, you interrupted me and said of the girl, 'I met her. She's a slut.'

YOU: That's not a word I'm proud of having used.

Of course not. But not ten minutes earlier, Trish had used the very same word with me—a word you know I hate—in precisely the same manner as you, with precisely the same inflection. A week later, when I found out that you two were having sex, the first thing I thought of was that word and those phone calls and the unavoidable fact that you two were already in sync. The affair, and its gravity, was so nakedly obvious in that moment. I felt like such a fool to have missed it.

YOU: I'm sorry for the way it happened.

Back when you and I were just friends—back when you were still playing in the band, still living with Holly—you threw a party one night.

YOU: Holly and I threw thousands of parties.

But I'm talking about Halloween, the night Trish was dressed as a zombie, and she and Holly ended up in the bathroom together. Holly told *you* that Trish declared her love for you, and Trish told *me*—later, when we were friends again—that Holly blocked the door and, crying, confessed to feeling unworthy of your love.

YOU: I know all about the bathroom. I heard about it from both sides.

There's a lot I never liked about Holly, especially the fact that she came in unannounced even after she'd moved out and I'd moved in, but I never thought of her as a liar.

YOU: She stole from us repeatedly.

She stole booze. She stole my makeup. She wasn't a liar. You disagree?

YOU: The truth is somewhere in the middle. Neither version could be totally accurate. They were both wasted. I was wasted. You weren't there. You went to bed so early. When we were only friends, I thought your early bedtime was quaint. When we were together, I found it aggravating and annoying and finally boring.

I've always loved the danger of night, of being awake when conventional people are asleep.

I also love being awake when it's dark out and most other people are asleep, but I love it in the morning when I'm on a long dark run all alone. I like that subtle fear of being outside and vulnerable at the start of my day. In other words, I like to be sober for the experience.

YOU: Yeah, and certainly for me part of the joy is in not being fully myself, being altered by a substance. You never lied about your stance on children, and I never lied about my stance on drinking. I like the feeling of being a little bit fucked up. We spend the majority of our lives sober and lucid and working. For me, for my mind, it doesn't feel like it's truly unwinding unless I'm also a little bit loopy, which is a word that *you*, and not I, would use. But to answer your question, I think they were both telling the truth and they were both lying. I know for a fact that Holly had concerns about our different backgrounds. I was 'from a good family.' She was ten years older and an on-again, off-again heroin user. She had definite insecurities about that, and when she got drunk or high or drunk *and* high, she'd get maudlin. So it's completely possible that she'd have ended up in a bathroom sobbing to Trish. I doubt, obviously, that Holly barricaded the door. She wasn't a physical drunk. That's where I believe Trish probably took liberties. But did Trish profess her love for me? Which would very nicely align with and ratify your insistence that she'd been

gunning for me our entire marriage, our entire relationship, possibly even before she'd ever introduced
us . . . It's impossible to say for sure, but I'll tell you
this. I saw Holly right after our divorce. I'd moved
back to Charlottesville, and I was living with Trish.
I knew Holly was around, but I hadn't seen her
yet. Then one night I was at my parents' restaurant,
hanging out at the bar with Trish and a couple other
people, and in she walked. Trish was still uncomfortable with what we'd done and what people might say
about her screwing her former best friend's husband,
so she didn't stay to catch up. Holly and I talked for
a few hours. We talked a lot about you. Regardless
of what you may or may not believe, she was rooting
for you. She thought you were way too good for me,
and she was even happy for you that we'd gotten a
divorce, but she was sorry for me, and she was furi-
ous to hear about Trish. All this to say, that night at
my parents' bar, Holly wasn't remotely surprised to
hear that Trish and I were together. She told me again
about the incident in the bathroom, despite my protestations, and her story was the same. No details had
changed. So there you go. I've played right into your
conspiracy theories.

You actually told me about that conversation. You called me the
next day. I thought you were calling to tell me Trish was preg-
nant or something. Instead, you just wanted me to know that
Holly agreed with me. Trish would have hated knowing that
you called to tell me. You told me that, too. And we laughed
about it . . . It's funny—maybe in a miserable way? But maybe

also in a ha-ha way?—but I'm reminded suddenly of one of my favorite things to do with you, before we moved away from Chicago. I used to love to sit for hours at the bar at Big Star and make up sitcom ideas starring you and me as you and me. You remember this?

> YOU: Patrick and Hannah Buy a Farm, Patrick and Hannah Decide to Sell Pot, Patrick and Hannah Move to West Virginia . . .

Yeah, exactly, and we'd get really into them. We'd plot out the entire thirty-minute script, during which we portrayed ourselves as complete buffoons—pot sellers who've never smoked pot, farm owners who don't like the outdoors.

> YOU: One time, Hannah and Patrick decided to get a divorce. You remember that one?

We decided to split up, and then we proceeded, throughout the course of the hypothetical episode, to spend every minute together. We'd set each other up on dates and then we'd show up at the same restaurant and only talk to each other.

> YOU: We were very funny.

Well, we were drinking pitchers of margaritas, so we felt we were very funny.

> YOU: We were willing to make fun of ourselves, that was the whole idea. That's what made our sitcoms so compelling.

One time, we adopted a kid.

    YOU: And we took the kid to bars.

But the kid was like twenty-one or something.

    YOU: Which would have been so like us back then.

God, we were dumb.

    YOU: Yeah, but we were young, too.

And, for a little while, we were in love.

    YOU: We were. That's the absolute truth.

PART THREE

A CODA IN PIECES

1.

Elmer died in December, a year and a half after the divorce. A few weeks later, I sold the car I'd owned with my husband (the practical hatchback that could accommodate his many amps and guitars, not to mention the dobro) and bought myself another MINI Cooper. A month after that, I sold our house and most of the furniture in it—the bed, the dining room chairs, the kitchen table, footstools, planters, a set of vintage lockers, a much-loved leather sofa, and a neon light that read JUST SAY BULL, which had been the centerpiece of a story-and-a-half wall of books, one of the first purchases we'd made together in Lexington.

Everything I'd fought to keep—house, car, dog—was gone. Patrick was gone, too, by then, back to Charlottesville, where he'd moved to be with Trish, and where Trish, abandoning her husband and New York, had moved to be with him.

What weren't gone were the memories. I didn't want them, didn't cultivate them, didn't linger on them or go after them, but there they were. Little triggers everywhere.

At the closing on the house, for instance, the buyer said suddenly of its street, "Aurora! I've always loved the name Aurora!" and I immediately remembered Trish's response when we told her we'd bought a house in Kentucky.

"A street called Aurora," she'd said. "How romantic!"

I remembered marveling at her exclamation—*How romantic!*—finding it strange, enviable even, that she could locate romance in something so quotidian as a street name. Those words bubble up even now, so many years later, when I'm least expecting them—washing the dishes, folding the clothes— *How romantic!* I'll think, and there she is again, almost as if she never left.

2.

For instance, there is the Nordstrom Rack sticky tag on the insole of a now well-worn pair of Birkenstocks I'd had to buy in New York after I'd walked too many miles without socks in a new pair of boots, thereby wrecking the backs of my heels. I searched everywhere for any pair of even remotely stylish mules with a lift. A pair of open-backed Danskos just then would have seemed like a gift from the gods. But it was winter, and my only option was a pair of oiled Bostons, a style I'd last worn in ninth grade—the platypus of the shoe family.

I hated wearing them later that same night as Patrick and I barhopped with Trish and George, celebrating the release of my second novel. I felt clunky and awkward next to Trish, who, as always, was in a devastatingly curated outfit.

At some point in the evening, between bars, she accused me, a little drunkenly, of exaggerating the problem with my feet. We ducked into a hotel lobby, and I peeled back my new socks to reveal my bloody heels, their missing skin, the bandages that wouldn't stay adhered.

"Oh my god," Trish cried, hand dramatically and suddenly to her mouth. "Now you have your official New York shoe story. Everyone should have a New York shoe story."

I'd marveled at that notion, just as I'd marveled at the romance attendant in a street name. It sometimes occurred to me that she used awe as a way to seduce me when she felt me turning distant. I am ashamed to say that it worked. Her flattery was addictive.

Occasionally, in the mirror, even now, I'll catch an unexpected glimpse of a mole on the outer perimeter of my right eyelid, and I'll think of Trish. She'd stroked the side of my face with her thumb one night. We were at a bar. We were drunk. We were almost always at a bar, and we were almost always drunk or about to be.

She'd said, nearly whispering, "I'm so jealous of this mole. So jealous. I wish I had something like this. It's not fair." I'd blushed, caught off guard by her compliment, and I remember wanting to find a mirror, even as I remember not wanting her to know how much I'd liked what she'd said and how she'd said it.

3.

Still other memories pop up more randomly, no traceable or obvious reason, as when I saw the plain gold band on Patrick's finger for the first time just after New Year's, when he was back in Lexington for a final semester of teaching. He'd asked to have coffee to catch up, and I'd agreed.

I suppose I was curious. From my sister and her husband, I knew that he and Trish had gotten married in Chicago the week before. I assumed he wanted to tell me himself, face-to-face, some kind of misguided act of integrity. Instead, he talked about the new book he was working on, lamented the current state of publishing, and complained about the laziness of his students. I listened for nearly an hour, waiting for when he'd tell me what I already knew, wondering if it would hurt to hear him say it, hoping I wouldn't cry if it did. But he never told me. He never acknowledged the ring.

Some days it floats into view, a small gold life buoy bobbing mindlessly along in the cloudiness of my peripheral vision.

4.

The night after I found out about Trish and Patrick, I started vomiting again. There was a moment during dinner—I was with Hugh and George, it was late, I'd finally started crying—when I knew I wasn't going to keep my food down. My eyes were already red; no one would wonder if they became swollen; and I knew that if someone in the bathroom heard me, if some unexpected woman confronted me—which was always a fear—I could tell her the *other* truth: that I'd just found out my husband was cheating; that the vomiting wasn't a compulsion but a reaction to what I'd learned.

Only one week earlier, I'd been at a bar with a friend in Kentucky. She couldn't stop going on about how unusual it was that Patrick and I were spending the entire summer apart.

"Do you worry about him?" she asked.

I understood her to mean *Do you worry he'll be unfaithful?*

My answer—as it had always been since the day we decided we were in love—was this: "No. Never. He could never cheat. He's incapable of keeping secrets from me."

I started vomiting again that night with Hugh and George because I could and because it was something that was mine alone and because it disgusted me and because it gave me anything else to think about other than the fact that I'd been wrong about Patrick; I'd been wrong about us.

5.

The next day, I took a crowded train from New York City to my sister's place in D.C. My cheeks were so puffed-up from crying that my eyes couldn't open entirely. Hugh had given me a travel-size box of tissues when I left his apartment that morning, but I'd gone through them before even getting on the train.

Somewhere south of Newark, I started blowing my nose directly into my shirt. I was aware of how I must have looked, especially to the man sitting next to me. I was also very aware of his suit, which was light gray with a slight sheen. I worried I would somehow get the fabric of his knee dirty—my tears, my runny nose, my general wretchedness—and so I pressed myself against the window and quietly sobbed.

At the 30th Street Station, the man stood up, and I stared hard out the window, my eyes raw, my face blotchy. I focused on my breathing. I focused on knowing the seat would soon be empty and I could be alone in my misery without an audience to judge me.

But before he walked away, the man put his hand on my shoulder. I gasped. I actually gasped, and then I looked up. He was looking right at me. I wanted to apologize, to shake my head, to explain that this wasn't who I really was.

"Whatever it is," he said, "it's probably going to be okay, and if it's not, there are probably people who love you." He got off the train, and I hyperventilated all the way to Union Station.

6.

That night, during the reading I gave at Politics and Prose, a woman raised her hand and said: "You write so well about trauma, but has anything really terrible ever happened in your life?"

Normally at these events I'm asked different versions of the same fairly innocuous questions. *Where did the idea for your novel come from? How long did it take you to write? When did you realize you were a writer?* As far as I can remember, I had never before been asked about my own proximity to misfortune.

In the audience were my mother, my sister, her husband (Patrick's cousin), and two of my former professors from the University of Virginia (both of whom had taught Trish and both of whom had been colleagues of Patrick's grandfather). Also in the audience was Isaac, Patrick's best friend since second grade, who'd been his best man at our wedding and to whom I'd grown close over the past decade. Isaac had texted while I was still on the train to ask if it was okay for him to bring his family to the reading as planned. He told me he'd just heard from Patrick about the affair, assumed I was feeling fragile, but wanted to see me anyway—he wanted me to meet his firstborn baby. Reluctantly, I told him yes.

There's a video of this reading online. A few months later— the divorce documents signed, Patrick's clothes and furniture gone—I watched it. I wanted to see what I looked like, a woman who'd discovered her husband's infidelity not forty-eight hours earlier.

In the video, my body language is relaxed; my eyes appear tired but not swollen (thanks, no doubt, to the hemorrhoid cream my sister applied for me when I got off the train). I am still wearing my wedding ring, which surprises me. With the audience I am casual, even funny. I make several jokes, and I laugh a lot. But there is a noticeable pause in my performance when the woman asks her question about trauma. Before answering, I look away from the camera and the crowd, gesturing offstage with my left hand, as though I am having a conversation with someone who isn't there, as though I am asking, *Can you believe the timing of this?*

Finally, laughing, I repeat the woman's question so that the rest of the audience can hear. My voice is hoarse and incredulous. In the video, I scan the crowd as I speak. I am buying time; I am looking for Isaac.

He'd arrived a little late and was standing toward the back of the bookstore next to his wife. I hoped he might give me a signal, some gesture of permission to tell the audience about Patrick and Trish. You can't see Isaac in the recording, but I remember his face, his sad smile, the way he looked down at the bundle in his arms as if to say, *But there is still goodness in the world, yes?*

In the video, you can watch me spot him. You can see the moment—a quick shake of the head—when I make the decision to instead tell the story of Pops's diagnosis, his prolonged and inhumane battle with cancer, and finally his death in 2006.

After the reading, Isaac and his wife found me. Together, they pulled back the edge of a blanket to show me the tiny face of their brand-new baby. My eyes watered instantly, and Isaac put a hand on my arm. I shook my head. I was unable to open my mouth. I was unable to speak or even to say goodbye.

7.

I met Trish in 2004, in a basement classroom of Bryan Hall at a meet-and-greet at the University of Virginia. She was in her second year of the school's MFA program in creative writing. I was a first-year. We were both there for fiction.

She wore yellow flats and bright orange lipstick. She had long red hair and dramatic bangs. She was very thin. I was instantly jealous of her looks and the easy way she joked with the other second-years, mostly men, and I badly wanted for her to want to be my friend.

My own looks back then were less fortunate. In April, when I'd gotten the news that I'd finally been accepted into my dream program, I booked a hair appointment and had more than eighteen inches cut off. The outcome was not good—even the hairdresser agreed—and so we kept cutting. At a certain point, there was nowhere left to go but home, and I ended up looking not unlike the Cincinnati Reds' switch hitter Pete Rose.

By the day of the creative writing get-together at Bryan Hall, my hair was an uneven chin length, and my bangs cowlicked up in the August humidity. I was wearing an unsuccessful pair of wide-leg trousers and a shirt that was probably one size too small for shoulders as broad as mine.

Before seeing Trish, and with the exception of my hair, I'd been mostly happy with my first-day appearance. But her bright orange lips, those yellow flats, that razor-straight line of bangs undid my self-assurance.

When I was called on to say something about myself, my cheeks burned fire and my neck turned a violent red, two ugly and involuntary symptoms of the situational rosacea I'd had all my life.

Later, when the meet-and-greet broke up, and we were encouraged by the professors to find our way to a nearby bar, where they urged us to get to know one another better in advance of the first day of workshop, Trish sidled up beside me.

"It's sweet," she said, touching my forearm with her fingers, "the way you turn all pink. You shouldn't be so self-conscious about it. The blushing makes you seem real."

She was three years younger than I was, and I felt like a little girl in her presence. That was how our friendship began.

8.

Alcohol brought us closer.

One night, when the bars were closing, Trish suggested we go back to her place. We'd been drinking beers and doing shots with an equine photographer she'd met at some bar earlier in the year. He was married but his wife lived out of state. Like Trish, the photographer had shown an extra interest in me, and their pleas for me to prolong the evening were convincing and seductive.

Trish called her boyfriend, the young trust funder, and told him we were coming over. He said he was wide awake and that he'd have a round of white Russians waiting for us by the time we arrived.

I've forgotten a lot of the things we said and did that night. I remember we sat around the kitchen table, playing card games and telling stories. I also remember feeling dangerously adult—up past midnight, drunk and vulnerable and burgeoning on becoming someone who could potentially one day be perceived as sexual.

At some point, we played truth or dare, and I chose dare.

Trish dared me to let her dress me in some of her clothes, and I experienced a flash of clarity during which I considered that the whole night had been an orchestrated mockery.

"You're so sexy," she said. "And you don't even know it."

I blushed because she was saying this in front of two attractive men. I blushed also because I wanted it to be true and knew that it was not.

"That's not a fair dare," I said. "I'm not your size."

"You're crazy," she said. "That's what I'm trying to tell you. You don't see yourself as you really are."

She was right, in that my body dysmorphia and my bulimia

were at an all-time high that first year of grad school. But she was also, quite technically, wrong. We were not and never would be the same size, in part because of my height and in part because of my build. I am taller and larger-boned. These are facts.

But her boyfriend and the married photographer egged Trish on, complimenting and begging me, and, after another white Russian or two, I let her take me upstairs to her bedroom.

The bedroom was a complete mess. Clothes were everywhere—heaped on the floor, hanging from open drawers, strewn across the bed, which wasn't just unmade but almost dismantled.

I come from a family who doesn't eat breakfast before making the bed each morning, who regards doing and folding laundry as a meditative and reflective activity. I was both charmed and horrified by this hurricane-aftermath of a bedroom.

Once we were alone, she told me to take off my clothes and then immediately started rummaging through her closet, taking dresses off hangers and adding them to the piles on the floor. It was a few minutes before she noticed I was still dressed.

"What's the matter?" she asked me. "Take your clothes off."

"You know those women," I said, "who leave towels wrapped around their bodies in locker rooms? Even when they're putting on their underpants? The ones who can put on a bra while still wearing the towel and who pull on their jeans before finally letting the towel fall?"

"The kind of woman who says 'underpants,'" she said.

"That's me," I said.

She nodded. She didn't laugh. She just handed me a bundle of clothes and said, "The bathroom is right through there. I'll wait for you. We'll go down together."

9.

My real understanding of that night of truth or dare didn't come until years later, until many of the previously very vivid details had already begun to fade. Trish and the married guy were having sex. Her boyfriend didn't know. I didn't know. His wife didn't know. I was the pawn who got him into the house, whereby he and Trish could continue to flirt under the nose of her boyfriend. I was the novelty distraction.

My presence that night might merely have been to serve the purpose of diversion, but it's also the night that solidified my friendship with Trish. We started spending more and more time together. Sometimes we still hung out at bars, sure, but after that night in her bedroom—when she hadn't made fun of me—we started meeting earlier in the day, for breakfast and lunch, at coffee shops to sit and write and read together. She loaned me books. She read my stories. She got me a job waiting tables. She introduced me to townies. Sometimes she'd show up at my apartment unannounced with a piece of clothing she'd just bought because she thought I'd look good in it. She was my first real adult female friend.

But it wasn't until the summer of 2005, when my adoptive stepfather was diagnosed with pancreatic cancer and given six to twelve months to live, that I started thinking of Trish as my best friend. She'd lost her own father several years earlier, and her familiarity with my heartache was more effective, more useful, than the Prozac I would eventually be prescribed by the grief counselor.

Weekdays, I'd wait tables and attend workshops. Weekends, I'd drive four hours to the Eastern Shore and sit by my stepfather's bedside and help my mother around the house. Sundays I'd return to Charlottesville, often not arriving until ten or eleven at night because I wanted to eat dinner with my mother before leaving town.

Trish would always wait up for me. We'd go to a bar. I could talk or not talk about my weekend, and her attention was always the same. If we were out in public, and I spontaneously started crying, she'd tell me to go home, that she'd settle the tab, that I could pay her back another time. Or she'd take me into the bathroom, clean up my face, and ask me what I wanted to do.

Her unfettered attention and kindness made my life—and Pops's dying—manageable.

10.

I was also aware of a creeping competition between us.

By the time Trish graduated, she was dating a poet from the program who'd eventually become her husband. I'd broken up with Stephen Strange and given up jog bras. She wanted me to find a boyfriend, someone we could double-date with, and so she began cultivating crushes on my behalf.

She was a bartender, and she was striking, and she had very little trouble drumming up men for me to talk to, men she encouraged me to like. Often they were uninteresting to me, or I to them, but when she did introduce me to a guy with whom I might have felt a connection, she seemed suddenly to have a difficult time extracting herself from our relationship.

She'd text him, and then she'd tell me what he'd texted her in reply. She'd say, "I think so-and-so is busy tonight. He told me to tell you." She could also be downright flirtatious, getting physically in the way before I'd even had a chance to be alone with the person.

Every once in a while, she'd disappear for an hour or two with a guy she'd pointed out as someone I might go talk to, only to return, coy and submissive, asking to buy me a drink, imploring me not to tell her boyfriend what she'd done.

She sucked me into her life and her lifestyle. And I let her. Episodes of lucidity about her behavior toward me or her boyfriend or my other friends tended to occur at times of acute distress regarding Pops's fast mental and physical decline. I'd pull away, only to find that I needed her, wanted her. She was my balm and my diversion, even as her treatment of me as a possible competitor fueled my physical insecurities, which in turn escalated my various eating disorders.

11.

One night, over drinks at the downstairs bar at the C&O Restaurant in Charlottesville, where George tended bar and Patrick played poker, Trish and I were talking about our bodies.

Of mine, I said offhandedly, "It's tidy."

She spit out her greyhound and said, making no effort to hide her astonishment or disbelief, "*Tiny?*"

I stared at the wooden bar and willed myself not to cry. "Tidy," I said again in an almost whisper.

I was mortified, because I would never have called myself tiny. I was mortified, because Trish's response made clear that I was not.

12.

As a young girl, I didn't learn about my body. I didn't learn about sex. But I did learn—by way of parental proximity and natural absorption—that men would have sex with anything; that sex should be reserved for marriage; that women who had sex with more than one man were loose; that a woman's sexual partners were notches on a belt, and that notches were something to look down upon. I learned to be ashamed of my chest, my waistline, my thighs, even the length of my legs. I learned to suck in my stomach. I learned to throw up much of what I ate. As late in life as graduate school, I was still wearing a jog bra every day because I never wanted to be accused of being proud of, much less aware of, the fact that I had breasts.

13.

One time, just after I'd moved into Patrick's house in Charlottesville, Holly walked through the front door while I was in the kitchen. Patrick wasn't home. I was cooking dinner. Holly just came right in and started going through the downstairs coat closet, where she continued—despite my meek protestations—to store several of her outfits, though she hadn't lived in the house for more than a year.

I leaned against the doorway to the kitchen, a lamentable little apron tied around my waist, and watched as she picked through the clothes.

"That's mine," I said when she pulled out a particular jacket.

"Huh," she said, trying on the jacket anyway. "Fits me, though. Doesn't it? Because we're both tall."

I didn't say anything. With Holly, it was usually best not to engage.

She returned my jacket to its hanger and shoved several dresses into her purse. Then she picked up a belt that had fallen to the floor and shoved it on top of the dresses.

"That's Patrick's," I said of the belt.

She closed the closet door. "You know who it belonged to before it belonged to Patrick?"

I shrugged.

"Before it belonged to Patrick, it belonged to me."

"Okay," I said, still leaning against the doorway. I didn't care about the belt. What I cared about was keeping Holly out of the kitchen. Our alcohol was in the kitchen, and she always helped herself.

"You know why I broke up with Patrick?" she asked.

"I thought Patrick broke up with you."

"You know why I broke up with Patrick?" she asked again.

"Why did you break up with Patrick?"

"Because of how he treated women. Because of how he treats his mother. Because of how he treated me."

"Okay," I said.

"You watch how he treats you."

"Thanks for letting me know."

"Just watch."

"Thanks," I said.

When she left, I locked the door.

I never told Patrick about that exchange. I never told anyone, not even Trish.

14.

A few months after my divorce, my mother came to stay with me for a long weekend. I took her to my favorite restaurant. I introduced her to my favorite bartender. She had her first martini. We sat at the bar, which was a novelty to my mother, who'd only ever been wooed by men at proper, tableclothed dinners.

"You seem happy," she said, her cheeks pink with gin. "So happy and healthy since the breakup."

"Yes," I said, also drinking a martini, also flushed with the lightness of booze. "So happy, so healthy. I am so fine, fine, fine."

15.

But I was not fine. I was a mess.

Since Patrick moved out, I hadn't slept through the night once. My childhood fear of the dark had returned, a new, intensified version, grown-up size, just like me.

My grandmother had been afraid of the dark. She lived in a white brick mansion overlooking a tony park in the heart of Atlanta. She had burglar bars on every window. She would not drive after the sun went down. When I was little, and I'd spend nights with her, she'd take me with her from door to door, locking and unlocking and locking them back again. We'd check the side door, the back door, the front door, and the basement doors.

Most terrifying were the sliding glass doors that overlooked the driveway and the park. These you couldn't be sure were locked unless you opened them, and so there would always be a few seconds when the night air—and its high cries of insects, frogs, and cicadas—would filter in and around us, before she'd slam the doors shut again, listening for the click that would confirm, yet again, that they were locked. I learned to love and fear this ritual, my fluttering heartbeat ping-ponging back and forth between excitement and true terror.

One night, when my grandmother and I were watching television, a car pulled into her drive, paused, then backed up, turned around, and went quietly down the road in the opposite direction. I watched, six or seven years old, as she ran around the house turning off all the lights. We huddled under the kitchen table together as we waited for my father, whom she'd called before grabbing my hand and yanking me into the dark kitchen, to arrive and save us.

After my divorce, when I was living alone in a freestanding house for the first time in my entire life, it was not an irregular occurrence for me to beg Elmer to sleep in our bed, instead of on the downstairs sofa, which he preferred. Often, in the middle of the night, having been awake for hours, terrified, sweating, listening for noises, giving in to disturbing and violent fantasies, I'd creep downstairs and check the locks I'd already checked multiple times before bed. I sometimes felt like a burglar in my own home, like a person hiding from herself. The way I'd sneak down and quietly jiggle the handle to make sure it was still latched, almost as though I didn't want some other, better iteration of me—ideally one sleeping soundly upstairs—to hear me, to know what I was doing, to witness my paranoia.

Most nights, I took an interesting and possibly illegal and definitely sometimes nearly fatal combination of pills and alcohol in order to sleep through the night. Only once did I rob a tablet of trazodone from Elmer's prescription bottle. Crossing that line scared me, and I promised myself I wouldn't do it again.

16.

I made lots of promises to myself back then, many of them less successful than my determination not to overdose on my dog's anxiety pills. I promised that *tonight* would be the night that I wouldn't leave the computer on in bed next to me, some mindless Netflix show on autoplay for company in the dark. I promised I would not start vomiting again. I promised I would not steal an extra avocado from the grocery store. I promised I would not open a second bottle of wine. I promised I'd stop talking aloud to Elmer when I took him on walks. I promised I'd stop imagining his responses as though they were real. I promised I would make dates with friends again. I promised I would learn to trust other people.

"That's not sleep," my doctor said of the dangerous dosages that allowed for my occasional losses of consciousness at night. "That's passing out. You're not getting any of the benefits of actual sleep."

"It's better than being awake and terrified," I told her. "It's better than my brain Rolodexing its way through every awful news story I've ever read about a woman being raped or beaten or left for dead."

She recommended a therapist.

17.

The last time I'd seen a therapist—not a grief counselor—I was ten years old, and my parents were five years into a custody battle that would ultimately last an entire decade. Therapy then was court mandated, and over the course of twelve months, I saw nearly a half-dozen psychiatrists and child psychologists. My mother chose a few, my father chose a different few, and the court added a couple of its own to the mix. During that year, both my parents told me what to say and what not to say to the doctors. Only once, in chambers alone with a judge, was I asked what *I* wanted. I remembered what my father told me to say and also what my mother told me to say. I had no idea what I wanted to say, and so I said nothing.

18.

My new therapist gave me assignments. Some I balked at completely. For instance, she instructed me to order an entire pizza, eat only one slice, and then throw away the remaining slices. I didn't like the idea of wasting so much food, and I told her so.

But other assignments I followed, albeit reluctantly.

A poet had moved to town at the same time I was divorcing. We'd been introduced at a party, and she'd invited me for drinks on a few different occasions. I'd turned her down each time, always citing bogus preexisting obligations.

My therapist told me I should take her up on the offer. Our conversation—obviously not word-for-word, but honestly not far from it—went something like this:

"What if she doesn't ask me again?"

"Then you ask her."

"What if I don't like her?"

"Did you like her when you met her?"

"She was funny. But all my female friends have been funny. They've also been mean."

"Did she seem mean?"

"I guess not."

"If you don't like her, then you don't have to see her again."

"How do you tell a person you don't want to see them again?"

"You tell them just that, or you tell them nothing at all."

"Hm," I said. "I don't know about this."

"What's there to lose? What's at stake if you get a drink with this woman?"

"I get attached to her, confide in her, and then she turns out to be a backstabbing liar?"

"That's funny."

"Funny because it's happened to me."

"What's there to gain?" she asked.

"Weight."

"You're trying to make me laugh, which is a diversion technique of yours."

"But you are laughing."

"Let's say she's funny *and* she's kind."

"Unlikely, but fine. Let's say that."

"What's there to gain? For you?"

"I have trust issues."

"You're telling me."

"Are you making fun of me?"

"You gain a friend. At worst, you lose an hour of your day and you never have to see her again. At best, you gain a friend. People need friends. Women need friends. Women need women."

"This all makes me want to barf."

"You're especially wry today."

"I mean it, just thinking about inviting a woman for a drink like I'm some kind of well-adjusted normal woman who has *girlfriends* makes my stomach feel all wonky and wrong."

"I've given you an assignment."

"Blah blah blah."

"Same time next week."

19.

I started ninth grade without ever having considered the weight or heft of my body. Like any girl, I'd spent plenty of time looking in mirrors and contemplating my breasts, my hair, my face, especially my acne, which flared up randomly and with great enthusiasm, usually above my lips, but sometimes across my chin, cheeks, and nose as well.

But at thirteen, nearly five eleven, I was still a size two—sometimes a size zero—and my awareness of body fat was nonexistent.

Two years later, a junior at boarding school, I was puking up most of what I'd eaten, and I'd learned to shower at particular times of the day, when the hallways were deserted and the common bathroom was almost always empty.

There was a certain shower stall—in the corner, away from the door—with a loose drain that I could remove with my toes, giving me direct access to the drainpipe.

I did most of my vomiting in this shower, naked and with the water running. I'd taught myself techniques to reduce the noises of regurgitation. I never coughed when I vomited. It was a point of pride. And the water helped mask the little sound I did make.

Once, alone on a weekend in the bathroom of my boarding school's black box theater, which had a private toilet with a door that locked, I nearly choked on a loaf of anadama bread. I hadn't waited long enough for it to soften before trying to get rid of it. The event shook me, but not in the right direction. After that, I became very careful with my liquids intake, always making sure that I didn't attempt to empty my stomach too early or without enough fluid for a smooth exit.

20.

My therapist asked me if I had any ideas of what might have changed for me between ninth grade and eleventh grade; between being a blissfully unaware pubescent girl and becoming a body dysmorphic teenager suffering from severe anemia.

I didn't just have an idea. I knew exactly what had changed. But I didn't want to tell her for fear of what it said about me, about my judgment, about my taste in friends.

In the past, I had blamed my food issues on my parents' divorce and the resultant decade-long custody battle. I'd read somewhere that children who feel unmoored or neglected often look to establish control in dangerous places—they become cutters, they experiment with drugs, they starve their bodies. This idea appealed to me: that I didn't actually have a problem with my body, I had a problem with my parents' behavior; that I didn't really care about being skinny, I cared about being in control.

Perhaps there's a smidgen of truth to this narrative. But there is also another, more obvious answer to my therapist's question, one I'd never wanted to admit aloud.

I started boarding school in ninth grade and struggled the first semester to make friends. In retrospect, I suspect most of us were struggling to make the transition. But I complained of my unhappiness whenever I could, and my mother—concerned about me—made arrangements for me to move back home, where I would attend a day school the following year.

By the end of ninth grade, I'd started to adjust. I'd found a little haven of goofballs in the school's theater program. I was happy. I had friends. But by then the new plans had been made, and I let my parents unenroll me.

It was at the day school where I met a girl who I'll call Martha. Like me, she was a sophomore, and, also like me, she lived on the Eastern Shore of Maryland. Every morning, our parents, along with a dozen or so other Eastern Shore families, drove us to the parking lot of the Queenstown Premium Outlets on the eastern side of the Bay Bridge. There, we waited in our respective cars for the six-thirty bus that would ultimately drive us another forty-five minutes in to Annapolis, where our private high school was located.

After boarding school, day school was a letdown. But Martha was funny. She was short and pretty and had very large breasts. She was also a little bit cruel. She liked my sense of irony and the vintage clothing I wore on weekends. I liked her acerbic wit and the fact that, although older boys often tried to get her attention, she chose my company instead.

Martha, also like me, was very skinny. I might not have noticed this—as I said, I was supremely if not also naively unaware of the notion of *weight*, mine or anyone else's—except that one day on the bus ride home, a pretty blond freshman girl said to Martha, "You're so skinny. It's not fair. Both of you. Like, the skinniest girls at school." I understood this was a compliment, but I was also confused. The freshman, to my mind, didn't look any different from either of us.

That throwaway remark, likely made to win Martha's approval, possibly even mine, was a turning point in my life; it was the day I started paying attention to bodies.

Unbelievable or not, prior to this incident, I had not noticed that Martha consumed exactly one bag of Skittles during the day and nothing more. Instead of becoming concerned, instead of telling my mother that I thought my friend had a problem and needed help, I became embarrassed by my own dining routine. Before then, my day had started with two bowls of cereal. Before lunch, I'd drink at least one bottle of Snapple. *At* lunch, I'd eat a bagel sandwich, which I usually followed with a Snickers bar or a bag of SunChips or white cheddar popcorn. After school, it was not unusual for me to eat an entire Swanson pot pie as a snack.

I started skipping lunches. Because I was observant and because I assumed my mother was capable of being equally observant, I continued to pack a lunch. I'd simply throw it away when I got off the bus. Martha was supportive. She started bringing me bags of Skittles, and we'd compare between class periods who'd eaten more than the other. The day's winner would still have a few left when we boarded the bus in the afternoon.

From there, the obsession intensified.

I wanted to know what Martha ate for dinner. I wanted to know how she got away with eating so little when she was at home, when her parents were watching. Her solution, to my mind, was brilliant, and I quickly adopted it: I became a vegetarian.

By the time summer rolled around, I was subsisting on rice cakes and boiled onions. If my parents took me out to dinner, where not ordering and eating a meal was too apparent, I vomited. The first time I did it, I swore to myself I wouldn't do it again. Martha and I had made fun of bulimics. Bulimics were people who couldn't control themselves, and we were in utter control of our bodies and our lives.

As the summer went on, Martha and I naturally grew apart. While we both lived on the Eastern Shore, we didn't live close to each other. By then, I was slated to return to boarding school, and she'd acquired a boyfriend I didn't like and who didn't like me. The dissolution of the friendship felt inevitable and ulti-mately insignificant.

By the time junior year began, I was vomiting on a daily basis.

21.

My therapist was curious about my reluctance to talk about Martha.

"It's embarrassing," I told her.

"What's embarrassing?"

"Because it was all so avoidable. If I'd just had guts. If I'd just had a personality of my own. I was already skinny. I didn't need to lose weight. Neither did Martha, but she thought she did, and she made me feel I needed to as well. She was so encouraging. She made me feel special."

"Is there anything else?" she asked.

"To have been so overwhelmed by another person."

She nodded, but she offered no feedback.

"I think I must have really bad taste in women."

22.

The second-to-last time I saw Trish was the winter before she and Patrick got married. I'd agreed, foolishly, to meet them for drinks at the little French place.

I lied when Trish, sitting between us, asked if Patrick still called me or if we sometimes met for coffee when we were both on campus and she was out of town. Lying to her, and helping my ex-husband do the same, felt good. This was the same woman who'd sent me photographs of the two of them at a laundromat during their week together in New York—when I was still clueless, when they were already having sex. *All grown up*, she'd texted, and then included a picture of Patrick pulling wet clothes out of a washer and into a metal basket on wheels. *Our Patrick*, she'd written. *All grown up*.

After we'd settled our separate tabs, I offered to drop them off at yet another bar, a dive he and I had only ever been to once, on the day we put in our offer on the house on Aurora.

Trish sat in the front seat of the practical hatchback—a presumption that astonished me, though I didn't object—and out of the corner of my eye, I watched Patrick, from Elmer's seat in the back, as he stretched out his arm and gripped her shoulder. The gesture, as I understood it, was meant to be discreet, secretive even, but also comforting.

When we got to their next bar, Trish lingered, the passenger door open, her hand on the hood of my car. "Does this mean I can start texting you?" she asked. Her tone was light, flippant even.

"No," I said, entirely unprepared for such a question. "God, no. You can never text me."

She shut the door, and I drove home, marveling yet again. *Does this mean I can start texting you?*

23.

For a little while after the affair, George and I would text or talk on the phone. He was struggling much more than I was to make sense of the end of our foursome.

Once he called to cheer me up. "They're starting a band," he said. "Just the two of them. She sings. He plays guitar. They both write the lyrics."

"Thank you," I said. "Thank you for making me smile."

Once he texted to tell me he'd had a poem accepted by the *New Yorker*. I was proud of him and said so. I asked if I knew the poem, if it was one he'd already shared with me. He said it was new. He wrote: *It's about being caught off guard by your ex's marginalia.* Then he wrote: *Sad!* To which I responded: *Sad!*

Mostly when he called, I listened. But sometimes—if it was late enough at night or he was drunk enough—I'd snap at him or hang up on him altogether. I always felt bad after, but I told myself I wasn't interested in analyzing what we'd lost or what they'd done. I told myself I wanted to move on, and it wasn't my job to help him. I was done with Patrick. I was done with Trish. And if George couldn't understand, then I'd need to be done with him, too.

24.

Except I wasn't done with Patrick.

For another year after the split, I took his calls or made my own. By the time he was remarried, we'd quit the correspondence, but for a little while, it was almost like having my best friend back. Especially over the phone—when we could ignore the physical tension—I could feel close to him again.

Once, he called to tell me they were moving to Chicago.

"Chicago?" I said. "Chicago? That's our town."

I was laughing; he was laughing, too.

"I love that town," he said.

"You hated that town," I said.

"I hate every town I'm in."

What might have happened if he'd been able to admit something so plain when we were married?

"The problem," I said, "isn't Charlottesville."

"Of course the problem isn't Charlottesville!"

"Then why move?"

"Because this town is a dump," he said. "We're stuck in the past here."

"And in Chicago you'll be free of the past?"

We were nearly hysterical with our laughter.

"I'm my own worst enemy," he said.

"You know when you get to Chicago, you're still going to be you, and she's still going to be her."

"I know, I know," he said.

"Wherever you go, there you are."

"You're okay, though?" he asked.

"I'm okay."

It took us months to learn to stop saying we loved each other when we said goodbye.

25.

I wrote the first draft of my third novel when Patrick and I were still happy, broke, and living in Chicago. In those days, we made the twelve-hour drive around which the book's action is centered—Chicago to Charlottesville—about three times a year. I read the opening chapter aloud to him on the same day I wrote it. He was standing in the kitchen; I was sitting at the table. We'd returned from Virginia the night before, and I'd gotten up early, eager to begin a new project. He listened to these new pages attentively.

"It's good," he said when I'd finished. "Just keep going."

I was buoyed by his enthusiasm, which was usually hard-won but fair. He was never indiscriminate with his praise, and because of that it was meaningful. I kept writing, as much to satisfy my own compulsions as to impress him with the final product.

Sometimes at readings, people ask me whom I write for, and I usually give them the same canned answer. "Ann Beattie," I say, "because she taught me a new way of looking at the world." But for a little while, the truth is that I wrote for Patrick, because of how good it made me feel when he liked it.

26.

Another time, I called Patrick to tell him I was dating a guy, that I thought it might be serious.

"Is he good to you?" he asked. "Does he make you laugh?"

In a million years, I'd never imagine that Patrick—the man I'd once handed a tissue while we said our vows—would ask me these questions.

"Yeah," I said, choking on the word. "He makes me laugh. He's good to me."

"He's got a kid, right?"

"He's got a kid."

"Does he know how you feel about children?"

"I plan to break it to him over time."

"Tell him they're like dogs. People love it when you compare their kids to dogs."

There was a winter day in Chicago—we were walking Elmer along the shore; there were tiny breakers in the distance, hexagonal ice slabs all along the seawall—when I felt suddenly and urgently that I wanted a child. Not just any child, but Patrick's child. I wanted it to grow up surrounded by our books and by his big brain and by my weird family. I wanted it to know Elmer and to love Elmer and remember Elmer as its first dog. I wanted there to be photographs of a tiny baby and an oafish brown hound. I wanted those photographs to be my life. I experienced that desire as strongly and keenly as I've experienced any other intense feeling in my life. But by the time we got home, it was gone.

27.

Elmer was a boxer–bluetick hound mix. He weighed seventy-four pounds and had four white socks. He could catch, roll over, sit, stay, and shake. Road trips turned him calm. We could drive from Chicago to Charlottesville, and he'd ask for only one pit stop. Thunderstorms turned him anxious. As did lightning, heavy rain, hotel rooms, swimming pools, empty houses, other dogs, and strange men. On the rare morning I slept past eight, he'd stand on my side of the bed and stare at me until I woke up. We called him The Creep, but he was our creep, and we loved him and treated him like a child. When friends told stories about their children, I'd respond with an anecdote about Elmer. To couples I didn't know well, I often neglected to point out that he was a dog.

"When Elmer can't sleep," I might say, "we put him in the car and go for a drive."

"Oldest trick in the book," some father might say back. "We do it all the time."

Elmer's mother, the boxer, had been one of Holly's strays. Holly was always picking up strays, and her strays were always having litters. I'd wanted to get a dog from the humane society; Patrick argued that Holly's puppies needed just as much help as any, possibly more. But I didn't want a puppy that would always, in my mind, be associated with Holly. I wanted disconnections from the ex-girlfriend, not reconnections. It was bad enough she still kept clothes in our house after so many years. I didn't want her thinking she had a dog there, too, that she could visit whenever she wanted.

Then I met the puppies, and I knew we'd be taking the fat one at the top of the pile home with us. I knew he was my dog. We called him Elmer T. Lee, after the bourbon.

28.

Nearly two years to the day after finding out about the affair, I got a postcard from George. It had been months since we'd last talked. I'd stopped answering the phone when he called. The conversations we had weren't worth the moment or two of utter loneliness I experienced after we'd hung up.

The picture on the postcard is of the Peter and Paul Fortress in St. Petersburg, a place I've been, a place I visited the summer before Pops got sick, the summer before Patrick and I started playing Scrabble nearly every day, when Stephen Strange and I were still a couple, and when Trish and I still swapped clothes and drank beers together late into the evening.

George's writing—handsome, confident—takes up all the white space. I read the note twice, then tacked it to the wall of my office. It's there still, along with a photo of Ann Beattie, a poem by Michael Drayton, a now meaningless scrap of paper in my handwriting with the words *beating heart cadaver*, and a receipt from my days waiting tables at the steakhouse in Charlottesville, at the bottom of which someone has written in red ink, *You are our favorite waitress!*

29.

Once, flying back into Lexington after Patrick moved out, I took a taxi home from the airport. I told the man which roads to take and which roads to avoid. The man told me he didn't like it when people looked at their phones and then gave him directions, as though technology knew more than he did, as though their phones and not he had been driving these streets for years. I told him I hadn't been looking at a map. I told him I'd merely been texting my family, telling them that I had landed, telling them I was safe and nearly home.

He said to me, "All the same," and then he told me that the cab we were in wasn't really his, that it belonged to a buddy in Louisville. He watched me by way of the rearview mirror when he said this, and I had a sense that I was being tested.

I wanted then to look again at my phone, but I felt I didn't have permission. I felt that looking at my phone would provoke an additional irritation in this man, and I wished like hell that I had actually been texting my family instead of looking at the traffic on my phone's map, just as he'd suspected. I wished that anybody knew where I was. More than anything, I wished for there to be someone waiting for me at my empty home.

When he finally dropped me off, he asked if I lived alone.

"No," I said. "My husband and dog live here, too." He smirked, and I went inside, my hands shaking.

I wasn't scheduled to pick up Elmer until later in the afternoon, but I called his daycare and asked if I could get him early.

Several hours later, just as the sun was setting, there was a knock on the front door.

Elmer barked, which was not unusual.

I was upstairs and, having showered, was already in paja-
mas. I wasn't wearing a bra.

The driver of the cab was back.

Because the front door was glass, he'd seen me come down
the stairs, and he'd seen that I'd seen him. I couldn't simply turn
around and pretend I didn't know he was there.

Elmer didn't stop barking, which *was* unusual.

I walked to the door but didn't open it.

"Can I help you?" I asked.

"Can you open the door?" he said.

"I can't," I said. "My dog is aggressive."

He looked at Elmer, and for the first time I realized how
large a man he was. Six five, possibly six six, easily 250 pounds.
I remember thinking, *This man could kill me*. I remember
thinking, *If I unlock this door, this man will slam me to the floor*.
It wasn't just a thought; it was a kind of all-body knowing, and
for an instant, I could see myself on the floor, feel him on top
of me. I shuddered.

"That dog looks mighty nice to me," he said.

By then, Elmer had assumed a low and constant growl.

"Can I help you? Is there something you need?"

"Your charge didn't go through," he said.

"Excuse me?"

"Your charge didn't go through. I don't get my money if the
charge doesn't go through. Can you open the door?"

Since getting home, I'd already begun an accounting of my
receipts, which I planned to turn into my work for reimburse-
ment the following day. I'd seen the charge on my bank account.
I'd seen the company name—Yellow Cab of Louisville—and
recalled the mistrust I'd felt when I saw it. He wasn't from Lexington. He wasn't a licensed driver.

"No," I said. "It did go through. I saw it."

"Ma'am," he said, "can you open the door? Maybe your husband can talk to me."

"I can't," I said. "I can't open the door. My husband is in the shower. But I promise. The charge went through."

Elmer and I stood there. The man watched us, and we watched the man, and all I could think about was the fact that I wasn't wearing a bra, the fact that he could see that I wasn't wearing a bra.

"I guess I can always come back," he said, finally stepping away from the door. "That's right. I can come back if the charge isn't there because I know where you live." He was smiling when he said this, and I knew he was enjoying himself, enjoying the fear he'd clearly evoked, the dread I would carry with me into the evening, into the next many evenings.

When he was gone, I called my brother, who was four states and twelve hundred miles away.

"I'm so scared," I said, nearly unable to breathe. "I am so fucking scared and alone."

He recommended a gun.

30.

For a couple years after grad school, while I was waiting tables and writing my first book, I taught an evening workshop for the extension program at the University of Virginia. My classroom was in a nursing building at the bottom of a steep hill. The nurses cleared out at night, about the time the creative writers went in.

There'd recently been a spate of rapes in the nearby neighborhoods—a few home invasions and an attack or two outside around tall hedges. It was an uneasy time for the women of Charlottesville, and we were constantly cautioned to travel in pairs.

After workshop one night, I stopped in the bathroom without asking someone to wait for me. When I left, the hallway was empty and dark. There was a single yellow light above the automatic doors of the exit. I stepped outside.

In front of me was the parking lot, also empty. Beyond that was the steep hill lined with hedges. At the top of the hill, out of sight from where I stood, were the more populated parts of campus. I started to walk.

A quarter of the way up the hill, which was unlit, I saw a dark figure with a high ponytail—a young female student of mine. I wanted to call out, but I couldn't remember her name, and so I ran after her, wishing desperately not to be going up that dark, steep hill alone.

The closer I got, the more aware I became of what I was doing: I was running after a lone woman on a dark hill surrounded by high bushes. I kept waiting for her to turn around, to scream, perhaps even to sprint suddenly away.

"Hey," I shouted when I was just behind her. "Hey!"

She spun around, her hand clutching at her chest.

"Oh my god!" she said. "Oh my god. You scared me."

"Why didn't you turn around? I kept waiting for you to turn around."

I was out of breath, my heart was racing, the sidewalks of campus were just ahead of us. People, in the distance, moved in groups beneath streetlights.

"I didn't want to be rude," she said.

31.

Fifteen years later, I still think about those words all the time.

I didn't want to be rude to the man at the steakhouse who only wanted to put the tip in or to a different man at the same restaurant who wanted—"only for fun"—to know the price of a hand job. I didn't want to be rude to Patrick by asking him not to go to another bar, not to respond to a text from an ex-girlfriend, not to have another drink, not to stay for one last song, not to bet another hand, not to *not* walk me home. I didn't want to be rude, because I was afraid of what might happen.

I like to say now that I have no regrets, that everything bad that's happened in my life—my parents' divorce, my decades-long eating disorder, my failed marriage, my doomed friendship—makes me who I am, and to undo or compromise or change any one of those experiences would be to undo or compromise or change me. And I don't want to be undone.

I like to say I have no regrets, but it's not true. Because I'd give almost anything to go back—to any one of those moments—to the man at the table full of men or to the female doctor who wouldn't sterilize me because she didn't think I—at age thirty—could have known my own mind or to Patrick when he was explaining why it wasn't a big deal that he'd gone alone to see Lucinda Williams with an attractive, single woman from his workshop and then gone out after, still just the two of them, until three in the morning—and be rude.

My god, to go back and be rude, just once. What a pleasure.

32.

I did not tell my mother, but I did tell my therapist, that I was considering having sex with a married man.

In college, I'd been indignant, outraged even, by the possibility of infidelity. I'd once overheard my brother say that people who cheated were cowards. That notion had landed with authority and rightness on my inexperienced and impressionable ears. It jibed with my vision of the world, which, back then, still a virgin at twenty, tended to view things as black or white, right or wrong, virginal or not virginal, etc., etc.

Then I got married.

Then I became unhappy.

Time turned my morals murky, and nuance seeped in. A good friend confessed her own affair. Rather than be incensed, I was amused. I asked for specifics.

In fact, by the time I agreed to marry Patrick, Trish had already acknowledged multiple infidelities of her own. One time, she'd been texting details to me from her phone while at work, and her husband, sick at home and using their shared computer, had read every word of our exchange. She texted me later that night. *George was watching*, she wrote. *Every word. He was watching! I am in so much hot water!* Her tone was playful. They stayed together. My lens by then was skewed. I knew I never wanted Patrick to cheat, and I was critical of Trish's actions even as I coaxed her for particulars. But I didn't take other people's adultery personally.

It was only after Patrick and Trish did what they did that I recovered my indignance from youth. Overnight, I became unforgiving of everyone's actions. I lost any sense of humor or desire to hear about others' affairs.

Then I met the married man.

He told me he was Australian but believed in the American dream and wood-burning fireplaces. I told him Helen Keller was our country's greatest con artist. He told me I was wrong: Anne Sullivan was the real grifter. Later, he looked me up online and sent me an email, ending the note with his cell number. In return, I sent him a text. He told me he and his wife had an agreement. I did not, for one minute, believe him.

We texted for two weeks, making plans and taking turns canceling them. He liked to call me *Hot Stuff*. I liked seeing those words in print. I assumed it's what he'd called every woman he'd ever had sex with. The likelihood of this didn't trouble me.

I liked to imagine him furtively deleting his texts, sneaking into the bathroom to read what I'd written. I liked that I didn't have to delete anything. I wasn't married anymore. I had nothing to lose and no one to answer to.

Over the course of those two weeks, I imagined what it would be like to pursue this path more seriously and to become the other woman. Would we meet at his house when his wife was at work? Or were houses too dangerous? They certainly seemed dangerous to me. Would we meet in his car? Would we drive to a nearby town? Would we take our chances and go to a student bar close to campus, where none of my colleagues ever went?

Toward the end, I considered the Australian's wife, who was a complete mystery to me. I tried to assign her a personality, deciding she was probably likable but not very funny. I gave her a hobby (avid cyclist), a baked good she excelled at (focaccia from scratch), and a friend in whom she confided but afterward always regretted having done so. Then I realized her husband had likely already had sex with her friend, and I never texted him again.

33.

Or maybe that's not true. Maybe I didn't think anything at all about his wife or her imaginary friend other than that the wife must be a little bit of a fool to be married to someone like that. And maybe because I thought they were both fools—he for being so obvious, she for being so permissive—it didn't make me feel bad to continue the texting thing until the one day we set a date and neither of us canceled, and I took him back to my place and then, only once there, only already unclothed and about to have sex, did I realize this wasn't something I wanted—he wasn't actually attractive to me—and so I walked him to the door. And maybe I was surprised by how easy it was and how easy it would have been and how—in the days afterward and then the weeks and then on the anniversary of the night when I almost but didn't have sex with a married man—I didn't once feel guilty about the fact that there was a woman, there was a wife, there was a *me* somewhere out in the world, not three miles from my house, in fact.

Sometimes I wonder if that's something Trish gave me, that sharpness, that cynicism, that dearth of common decency. Other times I wonder if it was there all along, the tiny black shadow that, years before Patrick's infidelity, caught me sometimes looking, wondering, hoping that there was someone out there for me who was better, someone who might, even while being married, tempt me enough to step out of myself, out of my marriage, just for a little while, just to see what it was like.

34.

There's a moment in *Listen to Me*, the novel that was published the same month Patrick and Trish began their affair, when the husband is parking the car. He sees his wife down the block. She's walking their dog. It's the middle of the day. She's wearing a robe. He has a sudden sinking feeling he is married to a loser.

In real life, I was the husband. Patrick was the wife. He was the one wearing the robe in the middle of the afternoon. But instead of wondering what that intense feeling of pity and repulsion suggested about me, about him, about us and our future, I wrote it down. I used it in my novel.

By the time the book came out and my marriage was over, I was able to see that I, and not Patrick, was the real loser. My hypothetical version of him was right. I shouldn't have said yes when he proposed. No one put a gun to my head and told me I had to marry him.

"Duh," I said when he offered me the ring.

35.

MY MOTHER OVER MARTINIS: I saw half a dozen erections before I ever had sex.

MY FATHER WHEN I WAS STILL A LITTLE GIRL: Look at those melons.

MY MOTHER OVER MARTINIS: I spent the first nineteen years of my life defending my virginity.

MY FATHER WHEN I WAS STILL A LITTLE GIRL: Look at those knockers.

MY MOTHER OVER MARTINIS: The truth is, I don't believe in sex.

MY FATHER OVER MARTINIS: Your mother will always be the love of my life.

MY MOTHER WHEN I WAS STILL A LITTLE GIRL: Suck in your stomach.

A WOMAN MY FATHER BROUGHT HOME WHEN I WAS EIGHT YEARS OLD: Remember this: *Sticks and stones may break my bones, but ropes and chains excite me.*

MY BEST FRIEND IN A LETTER: Being married is great, but I miss the lives that might have been. It hurts that I can't experience them, too.

MY HUSBAND OVER COCKTAILS: You're being paranoid. She doesn't have a crush on me.

MY BEST FRIEND IN A LETTER: When you're married, you're immune to excitement, and I hate that.

ANCIENT CHARLOTTESVILLE ADAGE: *You don't lose the girl; you just lose your turn.*

MY THERAPIST: It's no wonder you have difficulties with trust.

36.

Eventually, I got over my fear of the dark.

I didn't buy a gun.

I learned how to say what I wanted—out of life, out of breakfast, out of a friendship, out of a new pair of jeans.

I learned how to trust another person.

I learned to keep only the least important secrets.

Not a day goes by when I don't think about my relationship with food; when I don't struggle with some aspect of my body or with the knowledge—far, far back in my brain—that if I wanted to vomit up this particular meal or bowl of ice cream or slice of pizza, I could. I still start most mornings the way I started every morning of eleventh grade: my hands on my hip bones, grabbing, pulling, measuring for additions or reductions in fat.

The only difference is that now, when I think about vomiting, I tell my boyfriend, who sits beside me until the desire passes.

37.

The newly transplanted poet did invite me to get drinks again, and eventually I said yes. As it turns out, she is a very good person—one might even say she is an exceptionally good person—who is incredibly funny and also remarkably kind. She has a dog and a husband and is childless just like me. She drinks caipirinhas, and I drink margaritas, and we tell each other secrets, and I never wonder afterward if I've told her too much or divulged something too intimate.

It didn't happen overnight. During the early days of our friendship, I was wary, a stray cat hungry for the bowl of milk that's been left on a porch, but fearful that its tail will get stepped on in the process. I was always looking for her angle, wondering why she wanted to spend time with me, in spite of how much we laughed when we were together or how good I felt generally about life after we'd hung out.

But she wore me down, as good friends will do, with her consistency and compassion. Sometimes she'll send me a picture of a bird or a flower. Sometimes she'll text just to let me know she's thinking of me. Sometimes I worry that I am not a good enough friend to her or that she gives me more than I give her. When I feel this way, I send her a picture of my own—usually of a cactus, because cacti are my favorites.

Thinking of you, I'll say, and she always responds.

38.

And now it's five years later. By my own choosing, my life these days is governed by routine. I run forty-two miles a week in honor of being forty-two. I am vegan before six. I make my own pasta and bake my own bread. I own a house with a man who is ten years older than I am, who is reliable and serious and committed to stability. He believes in savings accounts and budgets, twenty-year mortgages and direct lines of communication, Sub-Zeroes and a quality wine collection. On Mondays, I run ten miles, and he rows 16,000 meters. Afterward, we order GirlsGirlsGirls burritos and make a bet about whether or not bicycle delivery will be available. Most nights, we go to bed by ten. Most mornings, we wake up before sunrise. Twice a week, we have coffee in bed, which is usually followed by sex. Our foreplay is the *Times* real estate section; we prefer homes in California for two million or more. At times, I am so predictable that I surprise even myself.

39.

But there are times when a phantom rage bubbles up, and the remembered knowledge—that I, a person who wasted so much of her life trafficking deliberately and even gleefully in paranoia and distrust, was duped by two people who were so close to me—threatens to undo me.

Last week, I chased down the driver of a Lexus coupe who'd run a stop sign and, in so doing, nearly hit me in the last leg of my morning run. I'd been feeling sluggish. It was meant to be a recovery run after a fast ten-miler the day before. When the driver, a woman, didn't stop, I shouted and threw up my hands. She turned, made eye contact with me, and then kept driving.

There'd been no register of shock on her face, no gesture of apology.

I watched her drive away. I felt sick with indignation and full of helpless rage.

Then I saw that, just down the hill, less than a block away, the stoplight had turned red, catching the offending Lexus.

I started sprinting, my heartbeat racing. I told myself, *If the light turns green, you'll let it go. If the light turns green, you'll just go home.* Other cars were pulling to a stop now, too. The light stayed red. I darted between a minivan and a sedan and came up fast and from behind on the driver's side of the Lexus.

I whacked her window with an open palm. "There was a stop sign back there," I shouted. "You could have killed me!"

The driver turned toward me slowly, her face completely blank.

I hopped back, sweaty and dazed, crazed with the excitement of having been wronged.

She rolled down her window.

Surely, I thought, *surely this person will now pay me the apology I am owed.*

Instead, her face turned ugly, her mouth a tight and nasty ball of red. "Lady," she said, "you're crazy. You came out of nowhere. You're a crazy lady."

I must have looked startled. I could have been laughing. "You didn't look left," I said. "You didn't even attempt to stop. I could be dead. Right now, I could be dead, and you would have killed me!"

"You darted out of nowhere."

"I was going six miles an hour!" I cried. "I didn't dart out of anywhere!" Certainly, I was smiling by then, the ridiculousness and the released rage feeling so good inside my chest, inside my belly. "You didn't stop! You didn't even look in my direction! You should be thanking me!"

"You're crazy," she called again.

"Thank me!" I begged. "You could have killed me. Thank me!"

I became aware of the other cars, of people rolling down their windows to listen. A man nearby yelled something indistinguishable, but I was surging with exhilaration.

"You're crazy, lady," she called one final time as the light turned green, as the car in front of her began to move forward. But by then I'd turned and was running toward home, running fast and feeling heady with vitality. I sprinted up my front steps, pushed open the front door, and called out to my boyfriend, "I HAVE NEWS! I HAVE NEWS! I HAVE NEWS!"

When I told him what had happened, he shook his head in amusement. "I thought you had real news," he said.

"No," I said, throwing haymakers at the kitchen ceiling,

jumping in place and then doing lunges around the island. "It just felt so good. It just felt so fucking good to be so fucking mad! It felt like . . . It felt as satisfying as my first conversation with Trish, just after I found out about the affair. I got every word right. I didn't stutter. I wasn't flustered. I was just right. And everything I said, I meant, and everything I meant, I said. It felt like that."

My boyfriend smiled at me and gave my ponytail a little tug. "I'm glad you got it right."

"I did," I said, nodding like some hopped-up actor from the eighties. "I did. I got it right."

For days, I raged with delight.

40.

During our first few months in Lexington, having left Chicago behind, Patrick and I rediscovered each other with the intensity of two people who've just started dating. We couldn't take our hands off each other. We were both getting up early, going to the gym, taking Elmer on walks together at dusk, writing for hours at a time, feeling like grown-ups, feeling like our real lives had finally started, and bills would always be easy to pay, and savings accounts would finally accrue, and our favorite bartender seemed always to be working the bar on nights when we decided last-minute to put off making dinner and go for a martini in the neighborhood.

One morning, during this magical era, I had an impulsive and powerful desire to hide under the sheets at the bottom of our bed. Three times Patrick walked right by me without seeing me, without knowing I was there. I felt the dizziness of childhood coursing through my bloodstream each time he walked by. But the longer I waited to be found, the less excited and more desolate I became.

Finally, after many minutes of lying there alone, breathing as quietly as I could, I pulled the sheets off and walked glumly down the stairs to our kitchen.

Patrick was drinking coffee and reading the paper.

"You didn't find me," I said.

He looked confused, and so I told him where I'd been and what I'd been doing. He patted the chair beside him. I sat down and tried to explain the melancholy I felt at not having been discovered. I told him that my brother and sister used to invite me to play hide-and-seek as a way to get rid of me. They'd tell me to hide, and then they'd never come to find me.

He put an arm around me and said, "But I found you. You're right here, aren't you? I found you, didn't I?"

For a little while, it felt that way. It felt like he had found me.

But the truth is, I was the one to find me. I'd lifted off the sheets. I'd gotten out of bed, and I was the one to say where I'd been and what I'd been doing. All he'd done was take credit.

41.

Patrick used to tell me that no matter where we were—in the car, at a bar, in the privacy of our own kitchen—I was only ever 25 to 50 percent present. The other half of me, he said, was thinking of a story or a novel I was working on, or replaying an anecdote from earlier in the day, or eavesdropping on a group of strangers in the restaurant booth behind us. I never objected to this observation because it was almost always true.

Only once—we were both a little drunk—did he tell me point-blank that my psychic absences bothered him. This was just before he was set to leave for our fateful summer apart. We were, as always, at a bar.

He said, "I wish you'd tell me more. I wish you'd tell me all the secrets you tell yourself all day long." We were both being so candid that night. We were about to be separated for three months, which was longer than we'd been away from each other in more than a decade.

I said, "I can't, though. You must understand that. If I said everything out loud, there would be nothing left to muddle my way through, I'd have no ambition to write, I'd have zero material, my instinct to tell stories would evaporate. I have to be like this," by which I meant insular, guarded, aloof. I paused. "I've *always* been like this. I *enjoy* being like this."

His response was so simple. "I know," he said.

42.

My boyfriend now jokes that I am feral—the way I snarl at unexpected compliments or bristle at an unanticipated kindness. He says that there is still so much of this domestication thing for me to learn, and he will have to teach me slowly, patiently, using compassion and sometimes the odd treat to convince me. After years of making jokes that other people's children are like dogs, I find that he is right, that I am the dog, I am the one who still has so much left to learn. And I am trying. Every day, I am trying not to assume nefarious intentions. I am trying to believe in the good faith of others. Every day it is hard. Every day it is easy to believe that everyone is hiding inside themselves, as I was for so long.

43.

The first time I saw Patrick, he was onstage. Trish had taken me to hear his band at a bar near campus. We'd gotten there late and had to stand toward the back. Patrick was wearing white pants, a vest, and a straw fedora. He was tall and thin and handsome in a boyish way. I was instantly attracted to him.

I knew, because she'd told me, that Trish had a budding crush on him. But Trish had George, and Patrick had Holly, who was playing the washboard onstage beside him.

"I don't think she's pretty," Trish said. "Do you think she's pretty?"

An older guy put an arm around Trish.

"Who's this?" he asked.

She introduced us.

He shook my hand and pointed at Patrick. "That's my boy. And that," he said, pointing at Holly, "is his bride du jour."

A little more than one year later—after Pops had died, after Patrick had recovered from brain surgery and broken up with Holly, after months and months of the two of us playing Scrabble nearly every day—that man, Patrick's father, would introduce me in exactly the same manner. And I'd realize, immediately, that it was how he'd introduced every one of Patrick's girlfriends ever. But I didn't want to be Patrick's bride du jour. I wanted to be something more than what every other girl had been. I wanted to be his wife.

For a little while, I was.

44.

The day before my thirty-eighth birthday, four months after our divorce, Patrick and I met for coffee. We talked about the dog, the house, his apartment, and the new car he'd just bought.

"You'll laugh," he said. "But it's the most independent thing I've done in years. It makes me feel like an adult."

I told him about some repairs on the roof that we'd put off but—because of a recent infestation of squirrels—I was finally having done.

He wanted to know if I was eating enough. "You look thin," he said.

"I don't know how to eat anymore," I said. "You've been the only chef in my life for the past ten years."

"You're trying to make me feel bad," he said.

"Yes," I said, and then smiled. "I miss your food. You're a good cook."

"I'll send you some recipes," he said. I told him to be sure to include chicken piccata and clam linguini because they were my favorites. A half hour or so later, we left. He went one way, and I went the other.

The next day, in my office mailbox, there was a single birthday present. It was a copy of Mark Bittman's *How to Cook Everything Fast*. He'd inscribed it: *Happy Birthday, Hannah, and Merry Christmas, and Happy New Year, and Happy Valentine's Day, and Happy Easter, and . . . With love.*

I walked into my office, closed the door, and sobbed.

45.

My boyfriend doesn't like it when I say it—I can see it in his face, read the drop in his cheeks, the shift in his shoulders—but the truth is, if Patrick had chosen anyone else, anyone besides Trish—the fictitious Cindy in Philosophy—I believe we would still be friends. I believe we'd be the kind of exes that Hollywood tries, mostly unconvincingly, to portray in summer rom-coms.

I've learned to stop saying things like this aloud. What's the point? But sometimes I really do miss him.

46.

Last night, I dreamed of Elmer.

In the dream, we are walking down an empty path. I can't take my eyes off him. I am so happy to be with him, this gallant and familiar animal. Every few steps, I bend down and make fists around his ears, ears as soft and silky as any lamb's. It feels so right, this walk toward nothing with my dog, with his four white socks and his kohl-black eyeliner. He is tall and awkward just as I am, except when he runs. When he runs, he is all grace, a gazelle of a dog. I am bubbling with delight, and it's all I can do not to lie down on the ground and hold him, and it's this—this idea of holding him tightly against my body—that reminds me he's gone, that I was with him when he died, that his head was on my thigh when he finally stopped breathing, his muzzle so still and so heavy. And then I realize I am dreaming. I realize he isn't here, he isn't with me, and I begin to cry. I am inconsolable, and that's how I wake up, crying and inconsolable in a bed that Elmer never had the chance to sleep on.

How long will he do this to me—show up and fill me with joy, only to go away again?

47.

I have a fantasy that in five years, maybe another ten, I'll be folding the clothes, doing the dishes, running up Shriners hill in the final stretch before home, and I'll think the words *how romantic!* but there will be no connection, no association with my past.

How romantic, I'll think, and I'll wonder where the phrase came from, what made it pop into my head, but there will be nothing there—a kite string without a kite, a leash without a dog, a costume without a child. *How romantic*, I'll think again, and I'll round the corner from Shriners onto Fontaine, and then from Fontaine onto Woodspoint, and I'll see my house, and maybe my boyfriend will be mowing the lawn; maybe he is waiting for me, watching for me, his hand held high in acknowledgment that he is mine and I am nearly home.

How romantic, I will think one final time, but the words will be meaningless.

ACKNOWLEDGMENTS

At various times and for various reasons, this book was made possible by the encouragement and support of the following people, all of whom are in possession of my lifelong respect and gratitude. I begin with Adam because this book wouldn't exist without him:

Adam Ross	Tim Wright
Ada Limón	Marlo Clymer
Blake Lenk	Noah Blue Sky Pittard
Michael Trask	Stacy Schultz
Stephen Trask	Greta Star Pittard Wright
Andrew Milward	Maria Massie
Cortney Lollar	Caroline Zancan
Emily Shortslef	Jeff Clymer
Fred Bengtsson	

I'm grateful to booksellers and book buyers everywhere, for the generosity of the Kentucky Arts Council, and to any writer who took the time to read and endorse this book early on. I'm especially grateful to the person reading this sentence right now: I hope there's a dog in your life who appreciates you as much as I do.

And, finally, to my family (you know who you are):

if you love it . . .

ABOUT THE AUTHOR

Hannah Pittard is the author of four novels. She is a winner of the Amanda Davis Highwire Fiction Award, a MacDowell Colony fellow, and a graduate of Deerfield Academy, the University of Chicago, and the University of Virginia. She also spent some time at St. John's College in Annapolis. She is a professor of English at the University of Kentucky and lives in Lexington with her boyfriend and stepdaughter.